To Janice

Just as the
pantry is inspiring
I hope this inspires
you too

Every success

Patricia X

# 7 Attributes for Success

## INNER SUCCESS & HAPPINESS

Patricia Elliot

authorHOUSE®

*AuthorHouse™ UK Ltd.*
*500 Avebury Boulevard*
*Central Milton Keynes, MK9 2BE*
*www.authorhouse.co.uk*
*Phone: 08001974150*

*First published by AuthorHouse 6/14/2010*

*ISBN: 978-1-4520-2771-5 (sc)*

*This book is printed on acid-free paper.*

# Contents

# About The Author

Patricia Elliot LL.B, M.Phil (Psyc), Post-Grad Education Certificate[1] is a leader with vision and values. She is a well-respected graduate of both Glasgow University and Strathclyde University with over 25 years experience in industry and academia in the fields of law, stress management and psychology. At a very young age, Patricia also studied and achieved LRAM and ARCM at the RSAMD in Glasgow, her instruments being piano, violin, composing and orchestration. With her knowledge and experience Patricia is now an examiner and author of Legal Aspects at the Chartered Institute of Purchasing & Supply[2] and Lead Examiner in MCBR (Managing Corporate and Banking Relationships) at the School of Finance (ifs)[3], involved in writing and validating examination papers and courses. Patricia is also a residential tutor in psychology for the Open University.

Her vision is to provide techniques and strategies to self empower and improve the lives of every individual. A daunting task you may think but Patricia looked back over her life and thought about how she dealt with different situations, particularly challenging ones. She also spoke with and listened to lots of

1    Patricia Elliot LL.B M.Phil (Psyc) PG Ed – for more information go to www.patriciaelliot.com
2    Chartered Institute of Purchasing & Supply (CIPS) go to www.cips.org
3    School of Finance (ifs) – go to www.ifslearning.ac.uk

people, hundreds, perhaps even thousands considering the span of more than 25 years - this is a lot of life and a lot of people!

Patricia realised that those who coped best, including herself, had certain attributes which they used to not just cope but also improve their lives. These attributes enabled them to look at their attitudes towards experiences, (past and present), and alter them in a positive way which helped them deal with things: work, home and life in general.

From her many interviews over the years it emerged that there were 7 core attributes. So the idea of a book was born. However Patricia believed that with the ever increasing use of the worldwide web people should be able to access tips and tools for understanding and using her '7 Attributes' to best effect to help deal with life's challenges. However, Patricia, as always, was ahead of her time. People could not understand how they could use a computer to help deal with life!! One person who shared Patricia's vision was her good friend and colleague Walter and although the web-enabled program had many names and was trialed and tested over the years, it will now emerge as Qvolution[4]. So look out for the web-enabled program.

Patricia has always had and continues to have a passion for books. However, she is also excited about the ever-growing worldwide web. With this combination of passions, Patricia is fulfilling a lifelong dream – a book followed by the web-enabled program Qvolution – a revolutionary approach to personal development and well-being.

Patricia recommends that an individual reads the chapters of this book sequentially especially if it is the reader's first venture into looking at personal development. However as we are all different, individuals can choose to read chapters that they like or need at that particular moment or just dip in and out as they will be able to do with Qvolution, the web-enabled program.

---

4   Qvolution – a web-enabled revolutionary approach to personal development and well-being. Watch out for news on <u>www.mindcircles.co.uk</u>

Participation in radio[5] and television programmes[6] and written articles for professional journals are sought as Patricia's views take account of both the legislative requirements for compliance with 'stress' health and safety as well as the solution through effective proven psychological strategies and techniques.

This book and the web-enabled program Qvolution to follow are dedicated to the select few who have 'gone that extra mile' and helped Patricia throughout her life, both in the happy times and in the not so happy ones and to say a big thank you to them for never giving up and believing in her, particularly when self-belief was 'low'. The time is now right!

Patricia also has a corporate vision - offering Qvolution to organisations particularly as the program offers a valid and reliable questionnaire as well as the personal development program for individuals – the ultimate life coach for the individual and the ultimate Employers' legislative compliance and preventative approach to stress. Information on Patricia and Qvolution is available on her websites www.patriciaelliot.com and www.mindcircles.co.uk

Patricia always welcomes constructive comments from individuals and hopes that readers connect with her and feel comfortable enough to contact her through the website www.mindcircles.co.uk.

---

5    Smooth Radio (previously SAGA radio 2005-2006) – Stress program
6    Teachers TV (2007) Stress project at Kings Langley School, Herts

## Acknowledgements

So many people have helped me throughout my life, both in the happy times and in the not so happy ones. There are too many to mention here but I must thank those few who have gone the 'extra mile' for me particularly in my times of need.

Those with vision have always supported me but less can be said for others, even my children, who at times have begged me to get a 'real job'. Fortunately as you will find out later one of the '7 Attributes' is resilience and thankfully I have this in abundance, certainly enough to ignore such pleas.

In recent years my oldest son, who of all my children has faced the most challenges in his life, has now turned out to be the most supportive.

Sometimes it is only when you are hit by hard times do you realise that you have to address what 'inner happiness' is and how to achieve it. As I sit writing this book my youngest daughter is facing life challenges and already I am seeing positive changes in her. She is focusing more on 'inner' well-being than 'material' wealth.

After a particularly challenging time in my life, when I was at a very low ebb, not certain what the future would hold, a colleague and friend, George Runciman, threw me a 'lifeline' – work as an examiner for various professional bodies. This set me on a positive path which brought with it further opportunities which enhanced and continue to enhance my life. So thanks George.

My friend Margaret Robinson has been there for me often night and day, making cups of tea, sorting, filing and just there as a listener. My friend Morfydd MacLaren has supported me emotionally and 'physically' with weekly tea and chats to keep me going.

My friends and colleagues Stuart Mallinson and his wife Anne have been positive motivators, providing very necessary emotional support and administrative/technical support of proof reading and copy editing, a daunting task particularly since I tend to re-write every time I review chapters or pages. Stuart provides the vital 'enough is enough'!

As a creative innovative person my head is frequently so full of ideas that I need 'grounding' from my many colleagues, too many to mention here but my grateful thanks to them all. The making of Qvolution has taken a number of years and it is hoped that the new version of this web-enabled program will be available soon. Thanks must go to Walter Taylor for his never ending patience, putting up with me for years and always ready to make changes almost at 'my beck and call'.

This book is written for everyone, family, friends, colleagues, all who know me, have met me, lifelong friends or passing acquaintances. Although I am unable to mention everyone here as the size of the book does not permit, those who have supported me will know who they are and whoever and wherever you are I thank you from the bottom of my heart.

# INTRODUCTION

*Life is too short to wake up with regrets... So love the people who treat you right... Forget about the ones who don't. Believe everything happens for a reason. If you get a second chance, grab it with both hands. If it changes your life, let it. Nobody said life would be easy, they just promised it would be worth it. Anon*

They say there is a book in everyone and that is probably true. However, actually writing the book is a different story. On my journey through life I have been asked many times for my book and even with this positive pressure it has taken me until now! So, I am probably no different from many other authors on that front! However, the time is also right for this book. It could not have been written without all my life experience and the many people who have contributed to my life both in a challenging way and in a positive way. I have to mention both because it is out of life's' many challenges that we gain our greatest strengths.

My confidence was also given a boost when I was asked to write academic books for the Chartered Institute of Purchasing and Supply[7]. Indeed when I was approached with the idea, my first thoughts were that I could not write such a book. It took my close friends and colleagues, Stuart and Anne, to point out

---

7    Elliot, P (2006), (2009) Legal Aspects in Purchasing and Supply

that the professional body must have had confidence in me to ask and know that I have the knowledge and expertise to do so. So I undertook and enjoyed writing these books despite it being challenging: particularly the tight deadlines. However it was the catalyst for getting to grips with writing my own business book and getting it published.

So why the 7 Attributes? Well, I looked back over my life and started to think about how I dealt with different situations, particularly challenging ones. I also spoke to and listened to lots of people, hundreds, perhaps even thousands considering the span of 'countless' years - this is a lot of life and a lot of people. However I realised that those who coped best, including myself, all had certain attributes which they used. I emphasise 'used' as I believe we all have these attributes but it takes 'hard' work and effort to use them!

Those who do so have different, more positive, attitudes towards experiences, (past and present), which help them deal with things: work, home and life in general.

In this day and age, we are overloaded with information. Of the many references to stress, (stress at home and at work) most are about the dire, resulting consequences to our health. I think that people (individuals and organisations) should be looking to prevent stress, not wait until after the event. It should not be a case of putting a sticking plaster on the emotional or psychological sore! Of course there are very real psychological problems which need to be addressed by professionals. However, for everyday living if you use the techniques, tips and tools in this book you can move towards a better way of being.

Of great assistance to me in writing this book was and still is my daily writing. Even at a young age I started writing a diary or you could call it notes (the length varies, depending on the issues, the time, whether happy or sad). Only years later did I realise that this is very therapeutic. Indeed writing things down is one technique I ask people to use, no matter whether happy, sad, traumatic, whatever. Research shows that it is helpful to actualise and this is one way of doing so. People worry about what they write or whether it has to be lengthy. I say don't worry how or what you write, it is for your eyes only and it can be as little as a few words or as long as you want or need.

There are other creative ways which are therapeutic, such as painting; writing poetry and similar. Again don't worry about how or what you paint or write it is for YOU and you alone, unless you want to share it of course but heed my warning below.

> *Tip: A warning about sharing your 'written' thoughts, feelings, emotions, negative or otherwise - remember never 'post' in haste!*

By this I mean posting on the internet or sending letters to others, particularly those who have upset or annoyed you. It may even have legal implications but often the person who has annoyed or upset you will not be aware that they have done so or even not be giving it a second thought.

By all means write things down but then put the email, notes or letter aside, or as your granny might have said, sleep on it! Another way of dealing with this is to 'throw' the letter away or rip it up.

Now you may be asking yourself why this book? After all there are hundreds, thousands of self help books written by all kinds of people. What is unique about this book? Well you could say because it is about my experiences and after all we are all unique. Another aspect is Qvolution, web-enabled program which is accessible through the internet using your unique username and password. The new version will be launched soon.[8]

This book and Qvolution are standalone. However one reason for the web-enabled program was because I recognise that many books just lie on a shelf whereas I hope that this will not happen with the combination of a book and a web-enabled program will motivate you to use the ABC core techniques and other tips and tools as part of your daily routine.

I want people to have access to strategies and techniques (through a book and my web-enabled program) which not only

8    Qvolution – to be launched via www.mindcircles.co.uk

give insight into some personal experiences, mine and others, but also one which is underpinned by psychological and scientific research. Don't worry I do not overload you with jargon.

Where appropriate I make reference to related research but I really want this book to be a 'friend on your shoulder' providing you with tools at your finger tips when needed or for daily use in improving your lifestyle. So many people work out their bodies but forget their minds! Maybe this is because they don't know how to work out their minds. Well there's no excuse now!

Another reason for writing this book was at popular request from those individuals who have heard my talks on the 7 Attributes and from those who have used and trialed the Qvolution web-enabled program for the purpose of the launching of the new version. There is much talk of stress management and I have designed and developed something which is much more. It is a stress prevention and management program as well as a personal development program.

Qvolution has many sections providing proven psychological strategies and techniques for everyone no matter who you are or where you are. So at popular request the new version is coming. It will have an online questionnaire which on completion provides you with a colourful graph showing the areas of your lifestyle which you need to work on. The questionnaire is not just about stress, but contains sections on general health, general stress, workplace stress (including the areas recommended by the Health and Safety Executive (HSE)[9], namely, demand, support, control, role, relationship, change). With the new version of Qvolution you will be able to complete the online questionnaire as often as you like, need or want.

In a climate where there is much talk of stress but not a lot of 'doing' (due to its difficult nature – stress is different for everyone!) and in an ever increasing technological age I believe that a web program is the answer. It enables people to talk more easily about stress (whether at work, home or everywhere) and as

---

9    HSE Management Standards relating to Stress (see www.hse.gov. uk)

the techniques are accessible to everyone, it can help individuals manage, reduce and even prevent stress.

However I want it to be more than this. I don't just want to look at stress I want to help people improve their lives and this can be done with the combination of this book and Qvolution.

The new version of the online personal development program will be available soon and accessible 24/7 any time any place via the internet. You can find out more about the online program and its benefits and by visiting www.mindcircles.co.uk or if you are interested in improving your workplace then why not speak with your Human Resource, Personnel or Health & Safety department personnel who can read more about the legal issues surrounding stress in the workplace or how to comply with legislation by visiting my website.[10]

Qvolution is also not just for the select few in any organisation. It is for everyone in the workplace from the Chairman, Senior Management to base level workers without whom organisations would not function. Being web-enabled it is also cost effective. So spread the word now.

At one time I did think that the program would be the ultimate personal development program – imagine - you can get tools, tips and techniques any time you want or need. However feedback from many people showed that a book had to be published too.

Now there is no excuse – you have the book. Look out for the new version of Qvolution – a revolutionary approach to well-being. What more can anyone want?

So you are thinking – where do I start on my journey to a better lifestyle? You are not alone if you are thinking this. Sometimes I think that people buy a book, particularly a 'self help' book and sit down and read it. However, unlike any other book a self help book is usually bought or wanted because it is needed at a particular moment in time. I have many self help books. Probably you have too. I have read some, bits of others

---

10 For legal issues surrounding stress in the workplace and general stress and how to comply with legislation go to www.mindcircles.co.uk

and so on. They then go on a shelf waiting until I need them and when I do need them I can't find the one that I want!! Does all this ring a bell?

By the time you are reading this I know you have bought my book. I do hope that it becomes your friend, there when you need it or just to read through. I hope that it sparks your interest in using Qvolution, the web-enabled program too because unlike a book which may get lost or dusty on the book shelf, Qvolution is there any time you want, need or like, any place!

Another difference between my approach and others is that I give you a reference point from which to start your journey. It is so difficult to start anything if you do not know where you have come from, where you are, or where you are going. Like finding a needle in a haystack. This is what the first attribute is all about.

However before finding out who you are the earlier chapters give information on my core techniques which I call my ABC. This is followed by a chapter on how habits are formed and then one on the causes and symptoms of stress.

Even if you are familiar with 'self-help' techniques I recommend that you read through the first four chapters to discover my approach and particularly why you should try to the ABC core techniques as a daily routine.

Then you start to find out more about my 7 Attributes. A chapter is dedicated to each of the 7 attributes and exercises are provided in the Appendix I at the end.

The first attribute is 'self-awareness' and is all about finding out who you are. Some of you may be thinking that this is a waste of time as you already know who you are. But I promise you, you are in for a surprise. Don't worry because unlike being appraised or sitting with someone else you can be alone. Just read the strengths and challenges and see if you recognise yourself. The reaction from lots of people when they do this exercise is to go into denial. However when prompted, and if they are open and honest with themselves they admit that they do recognise lots of the traits within themselves, negative and positive!

You will read about past conditioning and how we are 'labelled' - so another warning, do not use the exercise about yourself to 'label' yourself with these traits. You have probably had enough labels directed at you over the years (a whole section is dedicated to this!).

What I would really like you to do is to start looking at your life from a different more positive perspective.

Life is like an ocean. It is vast and uncontrollable. Many things are 'thrown' at you which are outside of your control. Often you may think that you are helpless to do anything about these things but you are wrong because even with things you have no control over you still have a choice as to how you deal with them. Later on a section looks at 'choices'. We all have choices, some good, some bad, some terrible but you can decide what you do and how you face these situations. Do you sink? Do you swim with or against the tide or current? Do you surf the waves? Do you sail through? Think about this for a moment and ask yourself what you would do.

> Tip: Although you cannot change the past you can change how you view the past and learn from it.

To do this can be frightening because you also have to be honest with yourself and you might not like what you see. All I ask is that you are true to yourself. You also have to take responsibility and be accountable for your actions. This does not make for an easy journey but then anything worthwhile takes hard work!

You are unique but like many others you may have had opportunities which you missed or had many life challenges and even suffered traumas. In developing this book I have drawn on my experiences in fields as diverse as drama, music, law, psychology, business and entrepreneurship. However more than all these different areas I have drawn on my life experiences and those of others.

I want you to understand that you are not alone in missing an opportunity or failing to learn from what life throws at you.

I have been there (too many times than I care to divulge!) but I realise that it is never too late. I continue to learn new things every day. You can do this too but you need to look at your life in a different way.

*If you lack the courage to start, you*
*have already finished.* Anon.

With much talk of stress at work and in life in general, I am approached more and more by individuals and organisations for solutions. When I suggest helping people improve their lives with on-going personal development I have been saddened and amazed at the reaction of some people, especially senior personnel in the workplace, who ask what personal development has to do with stress.

Fortunately many others get the concept immediately, some are catching on, others may never get the point but if I can touch the lives of some people then it will all be worthwhile. Your life is improved when you increase your self-awareness, self-esteem and confidence. I carried out research with a colleague at Queens University, Belfast[11] on the effectiveness of an online stress management program (which is now known as Qvolution).

Results showed reduced stress and absenteeism with increased self-awareness, self-esteem and confidence. This confirmed my personal experience. The research was presented at the British Psychological Society conference. The Abstract of the study *'Can Online Stress Intervention programs help?'* is detailed below.

---

11    Gibbons, C and Elliot, P (2003) *Can online stress intervention programmes help?* For more information go to <u>www.mindcircles.co.uk</u>

# ABSTRACT

*Cognitive Behaviour Therapy, Behaviour modification and Humanistic treatment interventions are long established, as is their increasing use through integrated, eclectic programmes. What is relatively new are attempts to offer such provision online. This study assessed the effectiveness of one such online stress management program (now known as Qvolution).*

I want to share some experiences with you, all its ups and particularly the downs as it is from the dark times of your life that you can learn more but only if you truly open your mind to the possibility of something different and even better. If you are able to do this then you will have the strength to go on, even in the face of great adversity. I know you will recognise, resonate and empathise with many of the situations described.

> *'From our greatest challenges we gain
> our greatest strength'* P Elliot

I would like this book to be your 'friend on the shoulder' to guide and assist, easily available in the happy and sad times. I have studied myself and many others over some 25 years. I wondered why even in my most difficult times people turned to me for help and advice. A phrase which comes to mind is 'go to Pat, she always has a smile on her face, time to listen'. When I think of this I can get upset because often it may seem that I had more time for others than myself or my family and many assumed or perceived that my smile meant I had no problems. Nothing could be further from the truth.

However, it was because of this phrase that I started to consider why some people fail or never seem happy, others succeed but are still not happy, and then there are others who no matter sad or happy, wealthy or not, are content and have inner happiness. I'm not keen on the phrase money can't buy you happiness because we do need money to live and of course it would be nice to have enough to always be 'comfortable'.

---

*Tip: Money is useful for a number of things, making you comfortable and helping you to extend help to others. Money may not buy happiness but it can stave off misery and make life more fun. It may and can make some choices easier.*

---

Bearing this in mind I decided to find reference points for people to identify who they are and where they are! At first I drew on my academic knowledge and experience and remembered the word 'ocean' as an acronym for personality traits.

When studying psychology many years ago I was introduced to the personality traits of Eysenck (1990)[12] and the research carried out by Costa and MacRae (1997)[13] which spell out the word 'ocean'. This also provides the connection to the sea (and I am Piscean!). The traits are:-

O - openness
C - conscientiousness
E - extraversion
A - agreeableness
N - neuroticism

I did not want to use the same words and I felt that the word 'neuroticism' was too negative for my liking. I am not too

---

12   Eysenck, H.J. (1990) Biological dimensions of personality. In L.A. Pervin (Ed.), *Handbook of personality: Theory and research* (pp 244-276). New York: Guilford

13   McCrae, R. R., & Costa, P. T., Jr. (1997). Personality trait structure as a human universal. *American Psychologist, 52,* 509-516

keen on negative words especially since many people are given negative labels by others when they are growing up. So I started thinking about all those people I have met over the years and decided that I wanted to have positive reference points.

I also realised that those who are successful in the non-material sense are those who have and use certain attributes. Hence the idea for 7 Attributes for Success was created and developed into Qvolution, my web-enabled program and this book.

# CHAPTER ONE

## Overview

*The pursuit of happiness is the chase of a lifetime. Anon.*

In this chapter I provide an overview of my tips and tools for success which I call my ABC; why systematic repetition is vital to that success; general information on stress and its effects and then a brief summary of each of the 7 Attributes.

I am very interested in how we use our senses. I use music and colour and this is reflected in the colours of the rainbow in the 7 Attributes which are:-

Awareness (self-awareness)
Resilience
Audacity
De-attachment
Encouragement
Value motive/respect
Know how

This overview is important for a number of reasons. It is to encourage you to read about some 'easy to learn and use' tips and tools, know what I mean by systematic repetition, have at your fingertips some general information on stress and its effects and finally have some brief information on each of the attributes. Of course each attribute deserves a chapter of its own!

My basic underpinning techniques which I call my ABC core techniques are easy to learn and easy to use. The ABC stands for Affirmations, Breathing and Creative Imagery.

You will learn more about these in chapter 2 but for now it is enough to know that affirmations are all about positive thinking, attitudes and behaviour; turning negatives into positives; seeing challenges as opportunities. B is for breathing. Now you are probably thinking well that's easy we have to breathe to live. However there are many different types of breathing and chapter 2 will provide more information on the more effective ways of breathing which will help you reduce and manage stress and help deal with life's challenges. The C is for creative imagery or some of you may know this as visualisations. You will learn more about visualisations in chapter 2 but it is worthwhile stating here that I have met many people whose initial reaction is that they cannot visualise. Over the years I realised that this is because visualisations often use words that do not 'fit' with everyone's idea of imaging. Don't worry about this just now as I give you different ways to try out in chapter 2.

To achieve success with my ABC core techniques you must practice and this is where my systematic repetition comes in. Only when repeated as often as possible, preferably when my ABC core techniques become part of your daily routine, will they work wonders for you - reducing, managing and even preventing stress. You can and will feel the benefit.

Systematic repetition is vital to the success of improving your well-being when using my techniques and strategies. You will find out more in chapter 3 but briefly it is all about forming good habits. If you are to succeed in increasing your well-being you need to have tools at your fingertips but more importantly for these to be effective the easiest way is for them to become good habits.

Now you know what I am talking about because you probably have some bad habits and we all know how easy it is to get a bad habit. All I am trying to do is help you to do the same for a good habit! More information on the importance of systematic repetition is discussed in chapter 3.

As for stress most people have read about it, experienced it in its many forms and we are constantly reminded about it. However I felt it important to include some information in my book because using my ABC core techniques and recognising the attributes and then using them can and will help you reduce and even prevent stress.

Before knowing how to deal with stress it is important to understand what stress is, how it is caused and what its effects are. With the ever increasing talk about stress you are probably stressed even thinking about stress! However I do provide information on the two faces of stress, both the positive and negative in chapter 4. I also provide some information on Qvolution – a revolutionary approach to personal development and well-being.

My book moves on to look at each of the attributes in turn. Chapter 5 discusses the first attribute – self-awareness. This is all about looking at how and by whom you have been conditioned in the past and then helping you to learn how to challenge this conditioning and your beliefs. Exercises are also there to help you form good habits.

Chapter 6 discusses resilience, the second attribute which is all about bouncing back against adversity. Pushing through the barriers of challenges.

Chapter 7 is about audacity, the third attribute. This is about being brave and courageous. It is about doing something new no matter how small. It might be to speak to a new colleague in the workplace or go somewhere different for coffee and smile at or say hello to the person serving you. It need not be something huge like climbing a mountain (although it could be!).

Chapter 8 is about de-attachment. This is possibly the most difficult to understand but it is one of the most helpful in dealing with relationships and people. It is not about being aloof or apart from others and it is not about being so dependent that you cannot be without the other person or other 'thing'. This chapter looks at jealousy and possessiveness which are the cause of many relationships breaking down. You will look at how to become more inter-dependent.

Chapter 9 looks at the fifth attribute - encouragement (and praise). You will learn how to start encouraging yourself and not to wait for someone else to praise you. Of course by learning this you will know and understand how important it is to encourage and praise others.

Chapter 10 looks at the sixth attribute – value (and respect). This is an important attribute and follows on from learning how to encourage and praise. There are many difficult people about and many may have had little encouragement when growing up. This chapter looks at learning how to value and respect yourself and earn how to increase your self-worth.

The last attribute, number seven is discussed in Chapter 11. This attribute is called 'know how'. Many will be wondering what I mean by this. It is not about being a 'know all' but it is learning how to ask when you don't know something or knowing how and where to find the answer to something you don't know.

Chapter 12 then summarises and provides an overview of the previous chapters.

There are many ways of reading a book of this kind. Some will read the book from cover to cover and then even put it on a shelf to gather dust. Some will read the chapters that they want or need to look at. However whatever your method of reading or having this book I want you to read it with an open heart and mind. I want you to practice the simple exercises. If you do this then I know that my book will help you along the way to a truly successful way of life, mentally and emotionally.

In the context of my book when I talk of 'success' I do not mean in the material sense (although this may happen when your well-being improves) but I mean in the highest sense of mental and emotional well-being, true inner success.

Life is not easy and it is harder for some than others: but then what is difficult or upsetting to one person may not be for another. You are unique and you may be looking for a technique or strategy that helps you while someone else is looking for another type of strategy.

> *It is never too late to become what you*
> *might have been.* George Eliot

No matter the strategy that you need or use, the core techniques which help every individual **when they are used,** are the basic tools which I call my ABC. If you practice these regularly (systematic repetition) then you have them at your fingertips everyday and especially at stressful times.

I hope you read my book with an open heart and mind, use my ABC and enjoy the inner success it will bring.

---

*Tip: start each day with a smile. As my mum used to say ' a smile costs you nothing'. Start now a step at a time.*

---

> *A journey of a thousand miles, starts with*
> *one small step.* Chinese proverb

**Exercise:** Before you read on you may wish to make some notes about what areas of your life you would like to improve or change in a more positive way.

(Notes)

# CHAPTER 2

# My ABC Core Techniques

*When it comes to well-being there is no
'I'll start tomorrow'. Anon.*

## 2.1 OVERVIEW OF MY ABC TECHNIQUES FOR WELL-BEING

This chapter discusses techniques which, if used and practiced, will improve your overall well-being. They will also help reduce and manage stress but only if practiced and used.

I call these techniques my ABC. I have practiced and used these techniques for many years and have found them to work. They were used in my research which showed that when using the core techniques self awareness, self esteem and confidence improved rapidly over a short period of time[14].

Although I have an interest in health and safety relating to stress, particularly, stress prevention and management my main focus is on improving overall well-being and the continuing improvement of personal development. As my ABC core

---

14   Gibbons, C and Elliot, P (2003) *Can online stress intervention help?*

techniques have shown to improve self awareness, esteem and confidence I like to think of them as my well-being techniques.

Furthermore I think that the word well-being is more positive than references always to 'stress'. Indeed some of the comments I hear and receive from people are that they are fed up hearing about 'stress'.

I know that if you practice and use my ABC core techniques then you can improve your overall well-being.

**WARNING! You can't just read about these techniques you have to practice and use them. You learn about practice and repetition in chapter 3 on systematic repetition.**

First of all you look at the individual techniques and once you know how to do them you can then learn to repeat them.

### BENEFITS
The benefits of using them include:-
- Reduced stress
- Increased energy
- Raised morale
- Enhanced self-esteem
- Increased confidence
- Easy handling of conflict and challenges

My ABC core techniques are designed to fit in with most lifestyles. If you practice them regularly then you will gain energy, confidence and enthusiasm. I know because I turn to these often and so do my many friends, colleagues and others I have met over the years. Those who benefit most use my systematic repetition method discussed in chapter 3.

Now I am not super human and I do get stressed and anxious at times – but not for long. I stop in my tracks and say – what about those techniques of yours! Indeed when I look as if I am getting stressed my family are quick to say 'What about those techniques!'

There are other techniques and self help books but in my opinion the ABC underpins most of them. I also like something that is quick and easy and that is what my ABC techniques are.

*They are as easy as ABC.*

As it is very difficult to get rid of bad habits and form new ones I also think it is better to offer something relatively simple which can become a good habit if practiced regularly. I know my ABC have benefited many people from the comments I receive.

One story I can tell you about starts with some negative comments about my ABC. One person told me in no uncertain terms that if something as simple as my ABC was going to fix his problems then I had another think coming!

Now I welcome comments particularly positive constructive ones. However I never ignore negative comments. So I investigated his negative comment and discovered that he was 'reading about' my techniques but not 'using and practising' them. When I tackled him about this he later told me that he had started using and practicing them and that they were making a difference to his life.

Of course remember that any technique (whether my ABC or others) do 'not fix problems'. What they do is to offer you the opportunity of viewing the problem in a different way. You will read in chapter 6 about the second attribute 'resilience' which is the ability to bounce back and to see challenges as opportunities. This is one of my strengths and it can become one of your strengths too. You may be so embroiled in a problem that you cannot see the opportunity that arises for you to learn from it.

*We cannot see the wood for the trees*

Now back to my ABC core techniques. Practice these regularly. Let them become part of your daily life - a good habit and you will maintain vigour and improved well-being. Even those who are physically ill find that the techniques can help with pain management and reduction. Of course every person is different and each individual will have varying experiences when using the techniques. Sometimes the benefits are immediate. Others will find it takes a little while before they experience the full benefits. I see this from the testimonials I get from people using the techniques. Read some testimonials in Appendix II.

So what are my ABC core techniques. In short they are:-

- Affirmations
- Breathing
- Creative imagery or visualisations

There are other techniques too and these are discussed later on in this book such as:-

- Remind yourself of your choices (see Chapter 5, Self awareness, Self Image and Choices)
- Reflect on and challenge your conditioning, beliefs and attitudes (read about this in Chapter 5, Self Image and Belief System)
- Control your mind, thoughts and emotions (read about thoughts in Chapter 3)
- Take action by doing something just for you
- Explore what is holding you back and do something that makes you feel good
- Relax (try the Q breathing exercise on relaxation later on in this chapter)
- Music CDs and DVDs to relax and unwind. Relaxing helps to increase energy, enhance memory, lower blood pressure, increase restful sleep and increase your sense of control.

I give you a starting point or reference point for you to find out who you are, where you are and what areas you may want to look at for improvement. In designing Qvolution I included in the stress risk assessment questionnaire[15] more than just what stresses people but how they manage and cope with stress. My good friend and colleague, Chris Gibbons, designed the managing stress and coping strategies sections which are produced in part below.

**Exercise:** Look at the list below and ask yourself if you do any of them to cope with stress?

- R for relax
- R for reviewing problems and trying to view them in a different way
- I for information. Seek out information to help you cope
- S for strength. Stop and recognise your strengths and what you have achieved
- S for support networks. Seek out appropriate support.
- E for exercise – physical exercise
- E for exercise – mental exercise (e.g. athletes reach the top by exercising both their bodies and their minds - why not try it)
- W for writing. Write about your thoughts and feelings
- W for writing. Write about a positive experience
- W for writing. Write about an unresolved issue
- A for action. Try to take direct action to deal with a problem
- L for laughter. Find time to laugh and enjoy yourself

**(Notes)**

---

15    Qvolution – for the questionnaire go to www.mindcircles.co.uk

Do you do any of the above? Do you do something else? Why not write down some of the strategies that you use. If you don't use any, write down which coping strategy you might like to start doing.

If you do something else I would be very interested in finding out what you do to cope with stress (nothing illegal please!)[16].

I am particularly fond of laughter, the last coping strategy mentioned above. It is probably the easiest and simplest of all but so many people do not laugh (or even smile). I remember a student from South Africa, while studying in Glasgow, asking me why nobody in Glasgow smiles. I thought for a moment and while I was thinking about what to say, she said 'I know why. They have to screw up their faces against the wind and rain!'

Now I don't know if this is the real reason but I was told from an early age that a smile costs you nothing so why not smile rather than frown. Indeed some research has been carried out over the years on the muscles one uses when frowning and smiling. The number does vary from article to article[17] with some saying you use 37 muscles to frown and only 22 muscles to smile and even some doctors saying you use 64 muscles to frown but only 4 to smile but all reach the same conclusion, you use more muscles to frown so why not smile and conserve your energy.

*A smile costs you nothing.*

---

16   Contact Patricia at www.mindcircles.co.uk
17   Daniel Goleman *A Feel Good Theory: A Smile Affects Mood'* The New York Times, 18 July 1989

## 2.2 'A' FOR AFFIRMATIONS

Now we will look at each of my ABC core techniques in turn. First of all my 'A' technique.

### A for Affirmations

The 'A' of my core techniques stands for affirmations. This technique is a powerful tool in combating the negative aspects of stress.

Although this technique sounds simple. It is simple but don't be fooled by its simplicity. It is very powerful and if practiced regularly you will take a giant leap towards a new way of thinking and a new you.

Using affirmations is a proven psychological method of improving overall well-being.

Successful sportsmen/women, business leaders and many successful and achieving people use this as a basic underpinning technique to their training.

Negative aspects are a very real part of your life, whether your own or those of others. Particularly nowadays stresses are seemingly increasing year on year. Your first small step to tackling these negative aspects and stresses in your life is to reduce and if possible eliminate any negative self talk. So how do you do this.

This is where affirmations can and do help if practiced. To best understand what affirmations are we start by looking at the definition of an affirmation.

*Definition:* An affirmation is a positive statement used to re-programme your subconscious. It is a statement when said to yourself, over and over, and with feeling, will influence internal forces and manifest change in your life.[18]

---

18    Emile Coue 19th Century French Professor

Affirmations are based on the following principles:-

- your present reality is a direct result of your thinking, so
- change your thinking and your reality changes
- affirmations change your thinking

Affirmations may also influence your immune system.[19] Richard Davidson's research found that a positive attitude can keep a person healthy. So it really seems to be 'mind over matter' even in illness. I make no apologies for repeating that one of the simplest ways of feeling better is laughter.[20] We have all heard the expression 'laughter is the best medicine' and for many years researchers have explored how humour helps patients relieve stress and heal. One research Melissa Wanzer[21] , Professor of Communications Studies at Canisius College, Buffalo, N.Y., has taken this research further. She looked at how humour affects the elderly and also how humour can increase effective communication in the workplace and in the classroom. Research is ongoing into the link between mental and physical well-being.

Although I appreciate the work of researchers in many disciplines I also believe that if something works for you, sometimes even if there is no scientific explanation, then why not try it and use it. I have found affirmations and the other techniques work for me because I have personally experienced the improvement in my overall well-being.

However I also know that it is important to know that research is undertaken and findings published on different aspects of psychology. What you experience when using

19  *Brain Activity Influences Immune Function*, Richard Davidson, Neuroscientist UW Jan 2003
20  *'Humour'* Melissa B. Wanzer, EdD, Professor of Communication Studies, Canisius College, Buffalo, NY *ScienceDaily (Jan. 26, 2008)*
21  Wanzer, Melissa B. *How humor helps medical professionals cope with their difficult jobs* Science Daily Jan 26, 2008

affirmations and some of the other techniques is an inner experience. The discipline of psychology relating to this is called Transpersonal Psychology. It is a discipline which provides a scientific language and framework for the research and reporting of the inner human experience. Abraham Maslow[22], founder of humanistic and transpersonal psychology theorised and documented aspects of human nature and human possibilities relating to personal perceptions and realisations.

Affirmations have long been recognised as a powerful tool in manifesting desires. This is because the subconscious mind cannot differentiate between actual reality and suggestions. Therefore it processes suggestions (or affirmations) as being 'real' and goes about using its powerful creative ability, and that of the nervous system, to make the affirmations become reality.

Scientific studies are also being carried which demonstrate that there is a link between mental and physical well-being. So those with a more positive emotional disposition may be healthier.

However, even regardless of any scientific research I say if it is simple to do, makes you feel better, then why not do it.

*Why be miserable when you can feel better!*

So how do you make affirmations part of your new habits?

The first step is as always, a small step. You start by making short statements. To ensure that these statements are effective I recommend that you follow the 3 Ps principle.

### 3 Ps Principle

- P for personal – this means that you should use the word 'I' which makes the affirmation personal to you
- P for positive – this means saying something positive and constructive

22   Maslow, A (1943) *A Theory of Human Motivation* and (1968) *Towards a Psychology of Being* and much more

- P for past or present (never future) – this means that you think of the statement as though it is something that has happened or is actually happening.

If this is your first time at using affirmations then you can use the simple affirmation below. There are many more and some examples are given in Appendix I.

One simple affirmation following the 3 Ps principle is -
- I feel good

You may not and probably won't <u>be</u> feeling good at the first point of saying this affirmation to yourself as the whole point of using this affirmation is when you are <u>not</u> feeling good. You say it, use it, repeat it to help you 'feel good'. You don't actually have to believe that it works, you just have to say it in to yourself 'with feeling'. You will start to see the difference.

---

*Tip: repetition is the KEY to the benefits of affirmations. Say the affirmation with feeling and repeat it 2 or 3 times in to yourself.*

---

I recommend this next exercise.

**Exercise:** Write your own affirmation on a small card and keep close by (in your wallet, purse, briefcase) to refer to as often as you can or need. Every time you feel challenged you can bring the card out and look at it and read and repeat. If this exercise is new to you, say your affirmation as often as you can, say 10 times every morning and every evening for the next few weeks. Soon it will become second nature to you and your way of thinking changes. This method of change is used in Cognitive Behavioural Therapy (CBT[23])

---

23  Cognitive Behavioural Therapy, Royal College of Psychiatrists link
    http://www.rcpsych.ac.uk/mentalhealthinformation/treatments/
    cognitivebehaviouraltherapy.aspx

This particular exercise may be new to you and if this is the case then I recommend that you try my 3-2-1 exercise (see Appendix I).

*Remember: practice makes perfect!*

**Exercise:** go to Appendix I and read about my 3-2-1 exercise. Then try to do this yourself in the space below.

(Notes)

## 2.3 'B' FOR BREATHING

*Whine less, breathe more*

Now we look at the second of the ABC techniques.

## B for Breathing

There are different types of breathing techniques and as a picture says a thousand words I am going to have short video clips on the different ways of breathing in the new Qvolution program and also on my website www.mindcircles.co.uk. My aim is to regularly update and have more video clips so please watch out for these on my website.

Now you may be wondering why my 'B' is for breathing after all breathing is fundamental to everyday life. So, breathing is really easy, right? It's something you do all the time without thinking about it? You have been breathing ever since you entered this world so why are you suddenly supposed to 'learn' a new way to breathe?

Well here's some news for you. You may not be breathing as effectively as you could or should. Most people do not take a deep breath, most people puff up their upper chest when breathing. So read on to find out how you can breathe more effectively.

Yes, everyone has to breathe to live but as I said above many people do not breathe as effectively as they could or should. Many people do what I call shallow breathing. This is breathing from the upper part of the chest. This uses up energy rather than gives energy.

**Exercise:** when you are alone in front of a mirror imagine you are at the doctors and you have been asked to breathe in and out. Now breathe in and out and watch what is happening to your body as you do so. This exercise is repeated in Appendix I.

**(Notes)**

Breathing more efficiently is important as it will increase your energy and you will feel better in body and mind. Efficient breathing ensures that enough oxygen is flowing to the muscles you are using and helps prevent unnecessary tension. Therefore, if you are practicing a relaxed full breath pattern it improves your focus and concentration.

When you are breathing efficiently, you expand your rib cage out to the sides and back without allowing your shoulders to lift. You also breathe into the lower part of your lungs where there is more efficient gas exchange.

Breathing efficiently is not as difficult as it may seem but it does require training of the mind and the breathing muscles. People who train as singers or in drama are usually taught efficient breathing techniques. Yoga is helpful as part of yoga involves the art of breathing.

**Exercise:** Another type of exercise used by dancers for years and one which has become popular and which you may have heard of or even taken part in is 'Pilates'. What about making a note to try Pilates or a similar type of exercise?

**(Notes)**

The Pilates method of exercise and physical movement is designed to stretch, strengthen and balance your body. It involves practice of specific exercises together with focused breathing patterns. Pilates[24] is used as a fitness exercise as well as an adjunct to sports training and physical rehabilitation of many kinds. However, don't worry if you are not training as a singer or actor and do not do yoga. You can learn techniques for breathing which improves your overall well-being.

Learning to do efficient breathing does not mean that you have to know all about how, what or why it improves your feeling of well-being but I provide some brief details here with some jargon but also summarised in user friendly terms. However for those who want to know more there is plenty to research on the internet.

Breathing takes oxygen in and carbon dioxide out of the body. However there is more to it than this. Breathing is only part of the processes of delivering oxygen to where it is needed in the body and removing carbon dioxide waste. The process of gas exchange occurs in the alveoli, which are the final branching of the respiratory tree and act as the primary gas exchange units of the lungs. The process operates by passive diffusion of gases between the alveolar gas and the blood passing by in the lung capillaries. Once in the blood the heart powers the flow of dissolved gases around the body in the circulation. As well as carbon dioxide, breathing also results in loss of water from the body. Exhaled air has a relative humidity of 100% because of water diffusing across the moist surface of breathing passages and alveoli.

To summarise in user friendly terms, when you breathe in you get more oxygen into the body by expanding the lungs from the bottom to the top to completely fill them. Oxygen is converted into energy. The oxygen goes into the bloodstream and this goes out to *all* parts of the body. When you breathe out the oxygen gathers *all* the toxins and takes them out of the body.

24  Joseph Hubertus Pilates (1883-1967) (New York) *Inventor and promoter of Pilates method of physical fitness*

Some of the benefits of efficient breathing include:-

- Relaxation and therefore reduced stress and tension
- Management of emotions
- Increased creativity
- Improved performance
- In meditation
- Improved well-being and overall health, and much more

I take a special interest in stress and stress related issues and promote prevention. I am particularly interested in some of the research on breathing which shows that lack of sufficient oxygen going to the cells of the brain can turn on your sympathetic nervous system, your 'fight or flight' response, and make you tense, anxious, irritable and even depressed. So if you want to avoid this, remember to breathe efficiently and through your nose.

Current television programmes like the Xfactor provide successful candidates with voice coaching. The voice coach will provide techniques for breathing because if you train someone to breathe correctly then they will naturally know how to sing. It does not mean they will necessarily sing in tune or win the Xfactor as there are many other factors involved but breathing efficiently is key.[25]

Efficient breathing techniques help you achieve different levels of sound. Such techniques also enable you to sustain the sound but more than that they help reduce tension and anxiety and your posture also improves.

*Tip: good posture cannot happen in your body if your neck and shoulder muscles are tense. You can improve your posture and feel more confident by breathing efficiently and by using specific breathing techniques detailed later in this chapter.*

25   Framingham study at the National Institute of Health Database www.ncbi.nlm.nik.gov/PubMed/

I was fortunate when young to be sent to elocution and drama. I was trained in breathing techniques which helped with voice production. I did not realise then that these techniques would enable me to remain calm and focused when required and also help me overcome shyness. Yes those of you who know me may not think of me as being shy but I was and still can be shy in certain situations. So there is hope for us all! I gained confidence and can remain calm under pressure. This has stood me in good stead in many other situations.

Others who benefit from efficient, improved breathing are champion athletes, opera and classical singers and those with ailments such as asthma. There are many clinical studies and research on breathing and you can find more information on the internet on 'breathing', such as, how it can ease conditions such as asthma and in some instances even reduce ad remove symptoms. Efficient, improved breathing can also help people who stutter.

In the world of musicians, breathing is very important to those who play wind instruments. Such players need to strengthen their primary breathing muscles and therefore need to exercise such muscles just like any other muscles. I remember when I was learning to play the clarinet my teacher asked me to check out my health as there was a change in my breathing. I discovered soon after this that I was pregnant. When I told my clarinet teacher, he said he had thought as much as my breathing pattern had changed and was shallower. I had to practice my breathing even more to strengthen my breathing muscles and indeed this training helped me prepare for the birth.

Many people do not breathe deeply and slowly enough. If you look at a child or a sleeping person you will see that during inhalation the abdomen blows out and during exhalation the opposite happens. This way of breathing is just the beginning. I say the beginning because a baby only breathes this way because its lungs are not fully developed. As adults your breathing tends to be the less efficient high chest breathing.

There are many sources of information on breathing and breathing techniques and I mention only a few above and those which I know have helped me. My intention is to provide exercises which I regularly use to help me feel better. If you use them you will feel better too.

There are other occasions when certain breathing techniques can help you maintain composure especially in 'public' situations such as funerals, weddings and other emotional occasions.

I admit that I am a very emotional person and openly cry at funerals whether of close relatives or acquaintances or in other emotional situations. However to maintain some kind of composure in public or at public events I use my 'calming' breathing exercise which helps maintain composure.

For this type of calm breathing is different from other breathing as it means I take a deep breath in through my mouth and then push my breath out through my nose. Any time I feel tears or emotion rising I do this type of breathing again. It is simple, quick and very effective.

Case Study: A Director of a company who had to give a public announcement about the unexpected closure of his plant was concerned about letting his emotions overwhelm him. He was and is a very caring man. He approached me for techniques to help maintain his composure. I advised him on the use of the ABC core techniques but showed him the 'calm' breathing which he should use just before as well as during the actual announcement I told him it is simple, easy to do and no-one would notice. I watched the television clip and was proud to see that he remained calm and composed with just enough emotion to show his caring side but remaining professional throughout. He told me later how much this technique had helped and that he would use it in the future.

> *Case Study: I took a group of my students to see a 'weepy' film. I divided them into two and told one group to use the 'calm' breathing when they felt tears or emotions rising. I told the other group just to watch the film. When we compared notes afterwards the group using the 'calm' breathing said that they had managed to keep their tears in check. They were surprised by this but even now they tell me that they use this technique when they feel their emotions getting out of control particularly when in public.*

Please remember however that it is not good to withhold emotions such as crying but at least with this breathing exercise you can do the crying in your own time and in your own 'safe' place.

As I said before a picture says and thousand words or a video clip says even more so to understand and learn how to breathe more efficiently so I will be putting short video clips on my website.

**Exercise:** read about the breathing exercises in Appendix I and then try them out. You need to use them, try them in different situations too.

> *Tip: efficient breathing helps you*
> * Be energised
> * Be calm
> * Be relaxed

Like affirmations, the breathing technique is simple but extremely effective.

So let us look further at the type of breathing that will increase your energy and help you to feel better.

Despite many people experiencing improved well-being through efficient breathing, there is still much confusion about healthy breathing and its related oxygenation. However I continue to breathe as efficiently as I can as I have experienced improved well-being and I want to pass this on to you.

I have mentioned before but I repeat here that breathing through your nose, or nasal breathing, is vital because your nostrils have hair and this hair acts as a filter for dust, allergens like pollen and other pollutants. If you breathe through your mouth then these particles go straight into your lungs.

**Note**: the 'calm' breathing exercise discussed earlier on is a short term type of breathing where you are asked to intake breath through your mouth but remember this is for a specific purpose and is not the acceptable way to breathe all the time.

When you inhale the abdomen blows out and during exhalation the opposite happens. So to repeat, when you inhale the rib cage expands and the dome of the diaphragm goes flat. This means that maximum air is brought into the lungs and gaseous exchange can take place easily, leaving the blood enriched with oxygen.

So to explain again, as you breathe out the rib cage collapses, the diaphragm is raised and the abdomen is sucked inwards. So in inhalation and exhalation there are 3 forces at work here, namely:-

Inhalation -
- Abdomen goes out (like blowing up a balloon)
- Rib cage expands
- Diaphragm flattened

Exhalation -
- Abdomen is sucked in (like a balloon deflating)
- Rib cage collapses inwards
- Diaphragm is raised

It is these three forces that ensure as much residual air as possible is expelled from the lungs.

When people are stressed they do the opposite of the above. They pull in the stomach while inhaling and push it out while exhaling.

Efficient breathing takes PRACTICE! The above slow rhythmic breathing is ideal for better oxygenation of blood.

**Exercise:** the Q-breathing exercise detailed later in this chapter and again in Appendix I energises, calms and relaxes. This may sound contradictory but it really works because although it increases your energy you do feel more calm and relaxed. Use as regularly and as often as you can. It can be good when lying down in bed just before going to sleep as it calms and relaxes. Make notes of what exercises you do, when, how, often, etc. Do not do this exercise while driving your car or operating machinery.

(**Notes**)

In addition to the regular energising breathing there are other specific breathing techniques which help in certain situations. Some of these techniques are explained below.

## FOCUS BREATHING (I use this to clear my head!)

I use this method of breathing when I need to focus or keep my attention so I call it my 'attention or focus' breathing. It clears my head!

This type of breathing is the psychological element of focusing and it helps get rid of tension. When you get rid of tension you will also get better at or improve whatever you are doing.

Focus breathing can be used not only when you need to focus on your work but also even in your leisure activities. Athletes use this type of breathing to clear their mind and focus on the matter in hand. If you are a golfer, try this type of breathing when you are about to take a swing, when you are approaching the ball or just do this breathing when playing.

The focus breathing is carried out by breathing from the lower part of your lungs to the top part (as in deep breathing) through your nose (remember the importance of breathing through your nose), keeping your mouth closed and then pushing out with a deep sigh – this empties the lungs of old, stale air. By doing this you are creating 'space' to enable you to fill up your lungs with new 'clean' air (or as clean as it can be in this polluted world!). Do this 3 or 4 times.

**Exercise:** read the above paragraph again and try to do the focus breath. – don't worry if you are having difficulty, just practice.

**CLEANSING BREATH** - the new Qvolution program will have video clips of different types of breathing. I explain how to do the cleansing breath below.

If you do yoga you probably know all about efficient breathing techniques and what is called the 'cleansing' breath. For the cleansing breath you take a normal breath in and then make short, rapid exhalations out of your nose (as if you are blowing your nose). You will feel your belly pulling in each time you exhale. Do this for about 20 or 30 seconds.

However for me my 'cleansing' breath is similar to my focus breathing. I breathe in deeply through my nose and then push out as much air as possible in short bursts through my nose before bringing in fresh air into my lungs. You can do this by following these five steps.

**Exercise: Cleansing Breath**

1. Take a deep breath in.
2. Now look up towards the ceiling and force air out through your nose with short sharp bursts. Do the short bursts in quick succession about 10 times.

3. Now look straight ahead and exhale forcefully as in step '2' to get rid of as much 'stale' air as possible - repeat 5 times
4. Then look at your feet and exhale forcefully as in '2' - repeat 5 times
5. Now take a deep breath in through your nose and relax.

**Exercise:** read through the above steps and try to do the cleansing breath. – don't worry if you are having difficulty, just practice.

## ALTERNATE NOSTRIL BREATHING.

### Exercise: Alternate Nostril Breathing

This type of breathing clears each nostril and allows new air to be brought into your lungs. Try the following five steps.

1. With the index finger of your right hand, close your left nostril
2. Exhale forcefully through the right nostril, now
3. Take your index finger off your left nostril and put the thumb of your right hand on your right nostril, close the nostril and exhale through the left nostril to clear out the stale air,
4. Do this 4 or 5 times alternating the nostril.
5. Then remove your right hand from your nostrils and do one or two deep breaths and relax.

**Exercise:** read the above steps again and try to do the alternate nostril breathing. – don't worry if you are having difficulty, just practice.

## FEAR & BREATHING

**Overcoming Fear Breathing.**

### Exercise: Overcoming Fear Breathing

Step 1    – stand with your feet a shoulder width apart
Step 2    – bend your knees slightly so that your body weight is supported by your hips and legs
Step 3    – lift your shoulders and then drop and relax them
Step 4    – let your stomach relax (don't hold it in!)
Step 5    – put your hands o your stomach
Step 6    – breathe in through your nose counting slowly to 5 and feel your diaphragm rise
Step 7    – breathe out through your mouth counting slowly to 5 and feel your diaphragm go in
Step 8    – stay relaxed and repeat steps 7 and 8 a couple of times more

Once you have mastered this exercise you can increase the 'count'. By regularly doing this you will be able to increase your slow count to 8 and even 10.

Benefit: you will be relaxed and yet alert.

Fear is a very powerful energy. It is the thought of what might happen. It can cause you to run at great speed and do things that seem impossible. Without it you would not know when to avoid danger. It is a necessary feeling as it teaches you to avoid dangerous things/people. So it is not something to be destroyed. However you need to understand and know when it is constructive or destructive.

---

*Tip: Do not avoid situations that make you feel uncomfortable; this only encourages fear to dominate your life*

---

The overcoming fear breathing uses all my ABC techniques together. Now I know my 'C' for creative imagery is not discussed until the next section of this chapter but it is worthwhile trying this exercise.

**Exercise:** Using all 3 of my ABC core techniques follow the steps below. I have put the letter of the technique beside the words so that you know what technique you are and should be using. This exercise is repeated later on once you have read about 'C' for creative imagery in the next section but try it just now.

- Imagine (this is using 'C') a fearful situation and ask yourself what you need to do to prepare for it
- Imagine (this is using 'C') yourself going through this situation positively and successfully (use 'A' for the positive)
- Breathe in using the efficient breathing technique (this is 'B') and be aware of the part of your mind that is fearful and that which is not
- Now ask yourself what is the worst thing that could happen
- Use an affirmation (A) - let yourself know that you are powerful and can over-ride the fear
- Use an affirmation (A) – say to yourself I have the courage to face this situation (or another positive affirmation which fits your situation – remember it must follow the 3 Ps principle which is discussed earlier in this chapter under 'affirmations'
- Breathe (B) in peace and calm and breathe out fear

Don't worry you are not alone in feeling fear and being afraid. The exercise below is one that can help you cope. Practice doing it and you will find that you cope better in many different situations.

**COPING BREATHING EXERCISE** . The new Qvolution program will have video clips of different types of breathing but meanwhile I explain this type of breathing below.

**Exercise: Coping Breathing**

- stand
- hands clasped behind your back
- breathing in, using the efficient breathing technique, raise your arms outward from your side and up to shoulder level
- bend forward breathing out, bringing your hands to meet at your feet, palms upwards
- breathe naturally to the count of 10
- breathing in, uncurl, keeping finger tips together, palms facing inward and in front of you until they are above your head
- then bring them slowly down to shoulder level and
- finally relax with arms at your side and rest.

**Exercise:** read through the steps above and then try the coping breathing again and then make notes on what other things you do to help you cope.

(Notes)

Once again, remember you are not alone in having fears. Everyone has fears but those who cope better are the ones who know how to handle them – that's what matters most.

**Q-BREATHING OR MY CALMING & ENERGISING BREATHING** This is repeated in Appendix I.

**Warning:** Do **NOT** do the calming and energising breathing exercise while driving a vehicle or operating machinery.

> *Tip: if getting or when angry or full of rage, road rage, similar: TAKE THREE DEEP BREATHS – this will calm you down.*

**or**

> *Tip: to calm down 'count to 10'*

You may have heard both these expressions before. Try one or both, you will calm down and your 'rage or anger' should calm down and even go away.

The 'tip 'take 3 deep breaths' was the tip given to the prosecutor by the judge in the O J Simpson trial when the prosecutor was losing her temper. It worked!

You may be wondering how an exercise can calm and energise. Remember the deep breathing calms and the oxygen going out and in is the 'energy'. So it is the intake of oxygen that energises.

The calming and energising breathing is best done when you are at home just before going to sleep or wakening up in the morning. You can do it lying on the floor or sitting in a chair.

> *Tip: for best effect practice this and try to take time to do this exercise everyday (and preferably even more than this).*

Considering how hectic life is for everyone, it is possibly best to do this in the evening before sleep. It is also worthwhile trying to close your eyes while you are carrying out the exercise.

Remember 'how' you breathe is important. Try not to breathe with the upper chest. Remember to breathe with your lower chest, expanding the rib cage, breathing from the bottom of the lungs to the top.

You can find out if you are doing this correctly by standing upright and placing your hands on your lower back. When you breathe in you should feel your hands move out, and when you breathe out you should feel your hands move in.

Many of my clients have told me over the years that they just don't have time for all or any of my exercises. I can understand how they feel but please note that this exercise takes about 58 seconds (just under 1 minute). I manage it in under 60 seconds.

It may seem longer and usually does because you are relaxed but I have timed it on many occasions while my clients are actually doing it and they are astounded at how short it is, yet feel as if they have been relaxing for many minutes. One client fell asleep and thought he had been asleep for half an hour!

**Exercise: Q-breathing**

Read the exercise below until you are ready to do it. Then try it with your eyes open and then once familiar with it, close your eyes and do it again. It is repeated in Appendix I. The new Qvolution program will have video clips but meanwhile the exercise is explained below.

| Body part | Approx Time | Procedure for the exercise |
|---|---|---|
| | | |
| Toes | 5 secs | Feel and focus on your toes by holding them tightly, then release and relax them, wiggling your toes |
| | | |
| Ankles | 5 secs | Pull your toes towards your head, focus on your ankles, hold for 5 seconds and then relax |
| | | |

| Legs | 9 secs | Stretch your legs stiffly, focus on them, firstly at the calf for 3 seconds then relax, then the knees for 3 seconds then relax, then the thighs for 3 seconds then relax |
|---|---|---|
| | | |
| Arms | 10 secs | Stretch your arms straight in front, pull hands and fingers together. Hold for 10 seconds and then relax |
| | | |
| Shoulders | 12 secs | Pull your shoulders up towards your ears. Hold for 4 seconds and then relax slowly, breathing out as you relax. Repeat twice. |
| | | |
| Face | 12 secs | Balance your head squarely on your shoulders to release any tension in the neck area. Screw your face up tightly. Hold for 12 seconds, then relax. Unclench your teeth and open your mouth slightly, relaxing it. Repeat twice |
| | | |
| Eyes | 5 secs | Lightly close your eyes, then tightly shut them, then relax the eyelids. This is the finishing part of the exercise. |

I, and many of my clients, find this exercise very helpful in times of stress and anxiety. I also recommend that you do it even when not stressed. I repeat my 'tip'.

> *A tip for quickly calming rage: if you feel anger rising, take three deep breaths or count to 10 and this is excellent advice as these tips give you a 'quick' time out.*

## 2.4 'C' FOR CREATIVE IMAGERY (ALSO KNOWN AS VISUALISATION)

*I am enough of an artist to draw freely upon my imagination. Imagination is more important than knowledge. Knowledge is limited. Imagination encircles the world.* Albert Einstein

This is the 'C' of my ABC core techniques. It is as important as the others for overall improvement of well-being and of course can be done at any time, any place. There are examples of my visualisations in Appendix I. I will also be putting them in Qvolution and even on DVDs.

I continue to add to the collection of scenarios and if you have any particular scenario you would like to see among the creative imagery then please contact me through my websites www.mindcircles.co.uk or www.patriciaelliot.com.

I am fortunate because I have always been good at imagining. Indeed some might say I had an over-active imagination. However it took me a few years of doing visualisations to individuals and groups to realise that for many people this technique seems or is difficult. I began to wonder why and feedback from individuals was often because they are called visualisations.

I started to think of it as creative imagination and this worked well for naming my techniques and it became the 'C' of my ABC.

We all have imagination, some use their imagination more than others. Sometimes you might be called a daydreamer. I say there is nothing wrong with daydreaming or any kind of dreaming. I try never to lose sight of my vision. Vision is different from goals. Your vision is really never ending. When you make or have goals the idea is to achieve them. When you have a vision it has no end. It is just 'there; always evolving and moving you forward.

The other difficulty by calling it visualisations is with the actual word 'visual'. Over the many years I have talked about creative imagery and worked through different scenarios with many individuals I realised that we do not all visualise or better still to use the word imagine in the same way. By this I mean the way in which you use your senses.

You have five senses (hear, see, taste, touch, smell). When the word visualise is used the tendency is for individuals to think or try to 'see'. When asking for feedback from those who have difficulty in visualising I realised that the difficulty was with the word 'see' in the visualisation. When probing deeper into the difficulty I started using different words in my creative imagery sessions. I asked individuals to 'think of' a time or place where they felt at peace, calm. I then used different words or asked them to use what 'word' suited the 'sense' they used the most.

For example, if this was the seaside. I asked them to remember when there were there and what they saw, heard, smelled etc. By doing this the individual could then create their own imagery.

**A hearing example:** if you use your hearing, the scenario for the creative imagery of the seaside might be – close your eyes, think of yourself at the seaside and hear the sea lapping on the sand or the birds singing above or the wind whistling in the grass.

**A sense of smell example:** for those who use their sense of smell, the scenario would be to smell the sea air, smell the fresh grass, smell the salty air and so on. Hopefully you now 'get the picture or should I say message'.

Another challenge for you as an adult is that creative imagery has been knocked out of you. Children have no problem in using their imagination. However as you grow up you are told to 'be in the real world'. Like me you probably remember being told not to daydream or to get real and so on. Well no more! You can take time and should take time for your own dreams. You can achieve great things through imagination. Champion athletes do!

*The great successful men of the world use their imagination...they think ahead and create their mental picture in all its details, filling in here, adding a little there, altering this a bit and that a bit, but steadily building - steadily building* Robert Collier

Creative imagery is not a new technique. Athletes and sports men and women all over the world use and have used it for years.

The effectiveness of visualisations was highlighted in a BBC Science television programme. The programme followed the training of a young 14 year old girl in her dreams of competing in the Olympics. The young girl was a gymnast and was learning a new move for her double bar routine. Her coach put her through her paces but each time she tried the new move, she failed to grasp the top bar. Now you would expect that continual practice of the actual routine would be the best way of improving. However she was asked by her coach to take time out and use her 'mind' to practice. Amazingly after repeatedly visualising the routine she carried out the new routine perfectly. This was a perfect example of visualisation or creative imagery in the real world.

The reason that visualisations worked for this young girl (and will work for anyone else) is that by repeatedly visualising her routine it was programmed into her neural pathways so when she came to physically carry out the exercise she had already mentally achieved it and therefore it was not a new routine.

*Tip: your brain does not differentiate between an imagined event and a real one. It carries out the 'programme' you have installed.*

You may have heard of and perhaps even used Hypnotherapy and Neuro Linguistic Programming (NLP). These are methods of mental training.

I talk of creative imagery because you can learn to do this yourself. There are those who may have a medical condition or addiction who should or will want to seek or require to consult medical professionals or therapists but for general improvement of well-being for most people you want the tools to hand that you can use to improve your well-being.

For me creative imagery or visualisation is one of the most powerful mental training methods used to transform performance. It is used by top athletes, trainers and successful people all over the world. Such people regularly but realistically picture in their mind the exact outcome they want.

Creative imagery shows time and time again to be successful in bringing major improvement to almost any area of athletic performance. So why not use it to improve areas of your life.

However for creative imagery to work most effectively you need to visualise when your conscious mind is relaxed as this opens up the link to the powerful subconscious mind. The images of what you want to achieve also need to be powerful, emotional and realistic.

You can or indeed may imagine or visualise all day but you probably don't realise that this unconscious visualisation can be and often is filled with negative thoughts. What you are actually doing is unknowingly visualising yourself to fail.

Athletes who experience recurring problems of failing are usually visualising in this way. What they need to do is to overcome their 'old' programming and change it with new programming in their mind.

Some of the benefits of effective creative imagery or visualisation include:-

- increased confidence
- increased belief in yourself and your ability to perform better
- reduced nerves and anxiety
- increased concentration
- reducing and removing negative thoughts and negative self-talk
- increased performance and positive results

It just goes to show you what imagination can do. Let your imagination guide you. The creative imagery technique applies not just to athletes but to everyone who wants to achieve their goals. Imagine yourself winning that trophy, going to collect your award or cup. Testimonials from my many clients show that my C technique does work. Read the testimonials in Appendix II.

Scientific Journals[26] have and are emerging that document the impact of visualisation in psychology, education, the arts and literature, sociology and much more. Physicists have begun to study subtle body energies and their effect on the world outside the body. Philosophers over the years have recognised this energy. The Chinese call it chi, the Japanese call it ki, the Indians call it prana.

I use it with clients and incorporate it into sessions in creative writing and problem solving. This is used in the discipline of education. It can enhance self-esteem and reduce stress.

> *Tip: when you need to do something well or something new, relax, visualise, and let it flow. You really will improve beyond your dreams.*

*The mind is a very powerful tool. Use it always.* Anon.

Even in academia visualisation has been and is used as a form of therapy.[27]

*Better still practice all three ABCs together and your life will change for the better.* Patricia Elliot

---

26  Journal of Mental Imagery
27  Johannes H Schultz *Autogenic Training* see also Samuels *Seeing with the Mind's Eye\*?*

## CHAPTER THREE

# Systematic Repetition – it's all about habits!

*It is notorious how powerful is the force of habit.* Charles Darwin[28].

Systematic repetition is all about habits. This is a vast topic and the information I provide here is not exhaustive. There are psychological articles[29] on the subject and many references on the worldwide web. As you can see from Darwin's quote the force of habit is powerful.

I do not want to focus on bad habits but it is easier to think about the bad habits because we all seem able to accumulate these more than any good habits. However instead of repeating

---

28   *Defining Habits,* Charles Darwin, The Expression of Emotion in Man and Animals (21)

29   *Habits: A Repeat Performance*, Neal, David T, Wood, Wendy and Quinn, Jeffrey M. *Journal of Association for Psychological Science,* Vol 15, Issue 4, pages 198-202
*Defining Habits, Dickens and the Psychology of Repetition,* Vrettos, Athena, *Victorian Studies,* Vol 31, 2000

your bad habits I want you to learn how to repeat your good habits (and eventually remove your bad ones).

Before learning how to repeat your good habits systematically you need to understand and know your habits, know how to stop the bad ones and how to form new good ones and repeat these so they become second nature, part of your everyday living. And as you can see from Aristotle's quote below, you can become excellent through repetition.

*We are what we repeatedly do. Excellence, then, is not an act, but a habit.* Aristotle.

It is through repetition that we form habits and I want you to learn the method of systematic repetition to form new good habits to improve your life.

**Exercise:** Take a moment to think about some of your habits. You may want to write them down in the space below. It doesn't matter whether they are bad or good habits. By writing them down you can look back later and see how well you have done. Perhaps you have stopped, removed or avoided them.

(Notes)

What did you think about, what did you write? The ones you probably thought of were your bad habits.

Now ask yourself why you have these bad habits. The answer is easy. You keep repeating the 'habit' whether this is smoking or eating unhealthily. If you want to improve your life then you need to replace your bad habits with good ones. Easier said than done I hear you say. Just think about all the New Year resolutions you make each year. You start with good intentions and by mid February or even earlier you have given up or perhaps not even started!

I hope that what you read here will help you to improve your life by getting, stopping and even getting rid of old bad habits and forming new good habits.

> *Tip: It is not what you read but how you act on the information given.*

The decision you make and the actions you take are yours. If you are finding it difficult then you can get support from the information in this book and by doing some of the exercises in Appendix I.

The first step is to become aware of your bad habits. This may sound easy if it is a physical bad habit such as smoking. The media constantly reminds us of the serious consequences of smoking on your health. Even so some people continue to smoke. However there are other bad habits which you may have and not be aware of because you perform them automatically, that is, without thinking.

Don't worry you are not alone. I have bad habits, indeed most, if not all, people have bad habits. After all we are human. The key is to become aware of them. Once you do this, you can do something about it. You can choose not to practice the bad habits and even learn and form new good habits!

When I was at school I learned to do arithmetic by repeating tables, for example, 2 x 2 is 4 and so on. Although there have been many changes in education in how we learn I can guess that the things you remember best are those you learn through repetition. This repetition applies to your habits both bad and good.

**Exercise:** Take a moment to think about your habits. Use the blank columns below – one titled 'good habits' and the other titled 'bad habits'. Now write down all the things that you do repeatedly and decide which are good and which are bad. Put the bad habits into one column and the good habits into the other. Use the space below to do this..

Good habits                    Bad habits

(Notes)

Just in case you had no bad or good habits here are some ideas. Some bad habits might be smoking, not exercising enough, drinking too much coffee and so on. If you get stuck with this exercise then I have made a list of different habits (bad and good) in Appendix I. You might want to look at my list (please note this is my list NOT my habits! The list is not exhaustive and you might even want to add some of your own habits. Habits will differ from person to person.

Don't forget to list your good habits. If you are having difficulty with identifying your good habits you can look again at my list in Appendix I. I am sure if you think hard enough you will be able to add to my list.

Obviously the habits you should be trying to stop are your bad ones. You need to learn how to NOT practice or repeat them. However you cannot stop the bad habits unless you know what they are. Therefore, you need to look again at your list to identify your bad habits.

Once you have done this you can set about learning to stop them. This is a daunting task and too much to do all at once. Therefore, you are going to take only one of your bad habits and think about how it is affecting you and those around you. How much time do you spend doing or using this bad habit? By doing this you can get to grips with the seriousness of the situation so that you can move on to improve things.

**Exercise:** Make a few notes in the space below on how much time you spend on the bad habit, who does it affect and so on.

**(Notes)**

Remember that good habits are your best friends, bad habits are your enemies. So why would you want to have so many enemies. Of course as I said above it is your decision to stop practicing your bad habits and your decision to take action. Therefore, you need to look at what motivates you to have these bad habits.

You need to ask yourself some questions about why you have any of the bad habits. Do you always argue because you want to be right all the time or are you afraid of challenges? Do you watch too much television to escape doing other work?

Already you may be noticing that some of the bad habits are 'physical' and others are 'mental' or 'emotional'. The 'physical' bad habits may sound easier to stop because you can probably identify them more easily and know that by doing something else you will benefit. However the process to form new habits is the same for physical and mental bad habits.

The process is helped by using affirmations. Look back at that section again and remind yourself what they are. I do hope that you are doing some affirmations.

**Exercise:** Look back at your list of habits. Can you identify which ones are which? physical, mental, emotional?

(Notes)

When considering why you have habits you need to look at how you have been conditioned in the past. Past conditioning is discussed in more detail in Chapter 5. For now just remember that by challenging your past conditioning and changing your beliefs and attitudes to more positive ones will improve your life.

As children you did not have the opportunity to choose your beliefs. When you are young you agree with the information given to you by others. You may rebel against these beliefs but when you are young you are not strong enough usually to win the rebellion!

When you are young your attention is hooked by others and you are introduced to rules and regulations by others such as your parents, teachers and other authority figures.

*Attention is the ability you have to discriminate and focus only on what you want to perceive.* Anon.

By using your attention you learn how and when to behave in society, what is good, bad, right and wrong. For example at school your attention is on what the teacher says. Such figures are all trying to hook your attention and through this you learn to hook the attention of others too so you develop a need for attention and this can become competitive, for example, you might become someone who seeks attention, the 'look at me' type person. Such behaviour continues into your adult life. This behaviour is selfish and is a bad habit.

Once you are aware of your bad habit and have considered the seriousness of the habit, looked at why you continue with this bad habit you then need to look at the consequences of this bad habit. The consequences will depend on the bad habit. For example if you are always argumentative ask yourself if this has an effect on those around you. Perhaps people avoid you or certain subjects when they are around you. Alternatively, are you domineering and colleagues at work find you difficult to work with and so on?

Everything you have been reading so far is about fact gathering. Once you have gathered the facts on your bad habits it is decision time. Only you can make the decision to stop practicing the bad habits. You have the power within to make this decision and to take action. Only YOU can do it.

Now you are probably looking at the long list of bad habits and thinking it's too much. You don't know where to begin. Well remember what I said earlier. You begin by looking at only one bad habit. With this one small step you can make a giant leap towards a better life. You can't change everything over night or even in a few days or months but you can make one small change at a time.

When you make the decision to stop one, more or all of your bad habits this is only part of the way forward. What you need to do for a better future for yourself and all those around you is to form new good habits.

In the same way that you formed the bad habits you are going to develop your good habits. How? By systematic repetition. You are going to repeat the new good habit until it becomes automatic. Use your affirmations to help you.

*You affect your subconscious mind by*
*verbal repetition.* D.H. Lawrence

This sounds easy but it is more difficult to actually do because the systematic repetition is not just once, or twice, but carried out for at least 30 days. There is much research on 'learning' and how to form new habits and the repetition process varies from 21 to 30 days.

For many years memorising and repetition were considered very poor learning techniques. However the value of rote learning is coming back and recognised as an essential part of good study practice. Repetition plays important roles in multiplication tables, touch typing, piano playing and many other subjects have long depended on repetition. It is therefore becoming clear that repetition can play an important role in any subject. Many e-courses on the internet make use of repetition to learn. Practice is all about repetition.

> *Any idea, plan or purpose may be placed in the mind through repetition of thought.* Napoleon Hill

Later on you will read about how repetition of an exercise using only the mind can impact on the outcome of the actual physical exercise.

> *Consistent use of new movement, processes, or postures provides a clue that learning is progressing* Mally, Kristi K[30]

I have experienced that if I want to form a good habit, the 30 day period of time works for me. Now by '30 day period' I mean that you must practice the habit regularly for 30 days. For example, if you decide that you want to form a habit of meditating then you start by doing this one day and repeating it every day for 30 days. I find that repeating something morning and night everyday is very effective and the purpose of my book is to help you to do this until the good 'habit' becomes second nature.

You will read later on about relaxing or energising exercises and one of these is a form of meditation. Indeed if you are thinking of forming new habits this is a good one to start with, especially since you can do this in your own home, possibly just before going off to sleep and repeating this every evening.

By now you are probably exhausted with all this information. However information is important for this is a vast and seemingly complex subject area but much more is available on the worldwide web.

Let's continue with the idea of forming the new habit of meditation. When you decide to form this new habit it will not help you to say to yourself that you are going to meditate everyday for life! It is better to say to yourself consciously (tell your brain)

---

30    Mally, Kristi K (2009) *Movement skill learning through repetition…* Journal for Physical Sport Educators

that you will try it for 30 days. Once you have meditated 30 days your conscious mind can choose to stop or carry on (or so it thinks!).

What happens in the 30 day period is that your neural pathways have formed. You will also probably continue with the new good habit as you will have seen the benefits and of course will want these benefits to continue.

A further complexity about habits is that there is a link between habit, thoughts and actions.

> 'Thoughts become actions, actions create
> habits and habits build character' or
> 'Watch your thoughts as they become words
> Watch your words as they become actions
> Watch your actions as they become habits
> Watch your character it becomes your destiny
> Therefore
> When your wealth is lost, nothing is lost
> When your health is lost, something is lost
> When your character is lost, everything is lost Anon.
> 'Change your thoughts, and you change your
> world.' Norman Vincent Peale

A book worthwhile reading is by James Allen[31] in which he discusses thought and character and the effect of thought on circumstances, health and body and the thought factor in achievement.

Psychology research on habits can be found in the area of 'learning'. According to an experienced flight instructor people fall back into old bad habits not because they cannot learn the new habit but because they cannot unlearn the old one!

I know there has been much to read and this is daunting. However everything worthwhile in life means hard work and

---

31    *As a Man Thinketh* James Allen (1864-1912)

after all you are going to make this daunting journey a small step at a time. Remember –

*A journey of a thousand miles starts with
one small step.* Chinese proverb

Another reason for taking small steps is that in the early stages of developing a new habit you will probably have more failures than successes and you can become disheartened for example when you give in to the temptation of having that cigarette after only the third day. You may just want to give up altogether.

However don't be disheartened because the key is in taking those very small steps towards your new way of life. Don't beat yourself up. In the early stages you need to remember that the key is to take small steps. These small steps take away the pressures and stresses that you might otherwise feel. Remember that what you are doing can be and is life changing but only for those who take action. Those with courage, act.

*If you lack courage to start, you have already finished.* Anon.

I have often tripped up or fallen after only a few small steps. You may find this too. This is usually because you have set yourself too difficult a goal to reach.

Like others, you may think that writing out lists and systems will help to support you and keep you focused on your new habit. However in the early stages of forming your new habit this can create problems as they will serve to remind you of your progress and of course in the early stages this often means reminding you of your lack of progress. So you end up getting anxious and stressed.

Experience shows that the more you focus on your progress, the more pressure you put on yourself. This is ok if you thrive on such pressure but if you make one slip you come crashing down.

Don't beat yourself up if you stumble at the first few hurdles. Pick yourself up, dust yourself down and learn from the situation. Don't be discouraged. Focus on individual days, and each day take a small step at a time forward.

> *Tip: Remain positive by using affirmations that you learned about in chapter 2. Doing this will also help you in your new lifestyle.*

**Exercise:** write down the one new habit you would like to form. Later on you can look back and reflect.

**(Notes)**

Remember then that you have to work out what is holding you back or making your efforts difficult.

> *Habit is habit and ....a bad habit.. is not to be flung out of the window by any man, but coaxed downstairs a step at a time.* Mark Twain.

*Example of repetition-based behaviour:* learning to drive a car. If you drive a car, try to remember what it was like to drive it for the first time. You might have been anxious or afraid. You certainly would have needed a lot of thought and effort to drive it. Your teacher provided support by talking you through the actions and being there with you.

Normally you would not be expected to sit your test after only one lesson. Therefore, you had more lessons. The reason for the lessons was to help the actions to become ingrained and automatic. If you have been driving for a while, think how different it is now after so many months or years experience. What was difficult to you then is now familiar and easy. This is because it is a habit – a repetition-based behaviour.

Habits are efficient and become second nature to you. This means you don't have to think too much about them. Some of your habits like rules and small rituals like washing, brushing your teeth are done one day and repeated the next and so on. Such habits can make you feel secure and help you through your day. Other habits might be your routines which help you organise your life. These can be positive provided you can be flexible when appropriate or necessary.

However not all habits are positive as you have seen from the lists you were to make of your good and bad habits. Some can be and are extremely harmful. Take habits that are addictions. These create dependency whether on substances, activities or relationships and these are harmful to you and those around you. Later on in chapter 8 you will read about the harm dependence can cause in relationships.

Other harmful habits are those which are self-defeating for example when you constantly create crises for yourself, such as continually being late or missing important commitments. You should want to stop these bad habits.

Think of your way forward as choosing not to practice your bad habits. Remember habits are patterns of behaviour programmed through repetition so you cannot change them but although 'old habits die hard' with practice the bad habits can be broken and even fall into relative or complete disuse.

## Practice make the master

Now a final word of warning.

You may, and in my experience you are more than likely, to be met with negative comments and attitudes from others, even more so from close family and friends. This is because many people are frightened of and do not like change of any kind even in someone they know and even where the change is positive for you.

You may also find your own attitude makes the decision to stop your bad habits difficult. This is where you may feel ashamed of yourself or feel bad or weak-willed if you slip back into an old habit. You must not feel this about yourself. Just understand that habits have a strong hold on your behavior.

*Remember a bad habit does <u>not</u> make a bad person.*

Focus on what you have achieved and take one day at a time. Just as it took practice to make the bad habits, it takes practice to break them. One small step and practice makes the master.

Positive thinking also helps and you already know this having read about affirmations earlier on in this chapter. If you need to remind yourself then go back and read about them again. Of course I hope you are already using them and that they are becoming one of your new good habits.

---

*Tip: A habit is only created because it is repeated! This is easy with bad habits. Now just do the same to create good habits!*

---

# CHAPTER 4

## Stress

*Qvolution – a revolutionary approach to personal development and well-being* Patricia Elliot

This book would not be complete without some information on stress. I know there is much talk in the media on this subject and many feel there is too much talk. However I have always had an interest in stress and what makes some people more stressed than others. It is also a subject which is studied by many psychologists. The information here is not exhaustive but I think it too important a subject to omit.

Furthermore I am keen to promote prevention of stress rather than waiting until someone is stressed and then do something about it. I designed Qvolution, a web-enabled stress compliance system originally for organisations which enable them to comply with health and safety legislation relating to stress. You can read about Qvolution on www.mindcircles.co.uk.

Qvolution is not a traditional approach of merely providing a stress risk assessment questionnaire for organisations. Qvolution includes 'the solution' in the form of a web-enabled program which aims at managing and preventing stress and is accessible to all employees. I actually prefer to call it a personal development program for the individual.

As I said above Qvolution was originally designed for organisations but as it was not a traditional approach to stress I found it challenging to get decision makers to understand the concept. Those organisations who have taken my Qvolution web-enabled service are ones who have Health & Safety Directors, Human Resources (HR) personnel and decision makers with vision.

I am amazed that many organisations and employers offer stress management workshops and courses believing that this is enough. Don't get me wrong, they are worthwhile and can be beneficial, just as the therapies offered by some employers to their staff are too.

However the traditional type workshops, training and the many therapies only reach a select few and sometimes only touch the surface of what stress is and how it affects individuals and the organisation.

Lots of people attending such workshops already know this information. What they are looking for are 'solutions'; techniques to help them de-stress and prevent stress in the future.

Even the 'train the trainer' programmes can cause problems to the employees not sent on the training. I know this is not the intention of such programmes but I have many stories to the contrary; of employees who are bullied by their manager and when the manager is sent on a 'train the trainer' program and returns, the bullying continues and even increases as the manager now has a higher opinion of themselves from the 'training'.

**Example:** more than a few clients have told me that their line manager is a bully. The situation became even more difficult when that manager was sent on 'week' training workshop. On their return their behavior did not improve and indeed became worse because they believed they now knew it all and started to 'speak at' employees telling them how and what they should be doing. The bullying behaviour continued and even became worse.

Continued bullying can happen and often does as the training is not used as a positive experience but to almost endorse the bully's perceived superiority. They now see themselves as better than others and use this to further bully when they return to the workplace. From all the stories and cases reported bullying is on the increase. Whether this is actual or perceived does not matter. It should not be tolerated. There are too many cases of bullying to detail here but more can be read about bullying on the internet.

My concerns lie with the media programmes such as 'Big Brother', 'Dragon's Den', 'Weakest Link' and the like where they think it is ok to speak to people aggressively and in a bullying manner. I am all for entertainment but in my opinion such programmes are giving off a message to people, especially young people, that it is ok to behave in this way.

So on the one hand there is media/press coverage and government legislation and regulations introduced to stop bullying behaviour and yet on the other hand more and more 'entertainment' programmes promote such behaviour.

Take a moment to think about these programmes and ask yourself if someone in your workplace has jokingly said to you 'You are the weakest link'. Now again I am all for a laugh and a joke but often this is the bully's excuse – 'I'm only joking' or 'Can you not take a joke'.

The problem lies in our being unique and much depends on what is said, by whom and when. I am sure you understand what I mean when I say that one person can say something to you and you take it as funny but someone else might say the same thing and you find it hurtful or abusive.

However if someone says something that hurts you and makes the excuse that they were only joking then you must not accept this. You must tell them that their words and behaviour are not acceptable. If you don't do this then the behaviour can and often does escalate.

**Example:** similar situation to the above but in this case most employees did get on with the manager. However the manager was sent away for a 'week' training and on their return the employees left in the workplace resented him having been away as the employees left behind ended up with his workload in addition to their own.

**Exercise:** ask yourself if you have ever had similar thoughts to the employees in the above scenarios. Have you ever thought when another employee is away on training and you are left in the workplace that they are away on a 'junket', that is, enjoying themselves while you are left behind to do your work and their work?

(Notes)

I am not suggesting replacing the traditional role of workshops and training but if everyone had the opportunity to access tips and tools to improve their overall well-being, their self esteem, confidence and more then it would make such traditional workshops and programmes more effective. My suggestion is to use Qvolution as well. So watch out for the new version which is being developed.

Sadly some HR personnel think that they will not be needed if their organisation takes up Qvolution. Nothing could be further from the truth. Qvolution would take the burden off HR shoulders as the stress risk assessment is completed online and because it is independent of the organisation more employees complete it. It is common sense that if a questionnaire is carried out in-house employees are reluctant to complete it, believing that their answers will be seen and known to the very people that may be bullying them. This of course should not be true and in many places will not be true. However as it is the employees' perception, completion of in-house questionnaires often remain very low.

Of course no matter whether the questionnaire is in-house or carried out independently people still want to know the results of completing the questionnaire. This is taking a long time in the larger organisations as it requires submission of questionnaires, collation of results, analysing of data and so on. Professionals have trained for years on how to frame questionnaires, collate and analyse data and yet many HR do or are expected to do this work.

Qvolution will do the work for them. It provides a colourful graph for the individual showing what areas they may need to improve. As you will have read in chapter 1 (the overview) Qvolution stress risk assessment includes the six sections required under Health and Safety Management Standards for Stress (demand, support, control, role, relationship and change) but more than that it has further sections on general health, general stress, coping and management strategies.

As I said above my original idea was to offer Qvolution to organisations but due to the many individuals asking for the program I decided to make Qvolution available to individuals. So the new version will be available to individuals shortly. Watch out for news. Subscribe to my Newsletter by going to my website www.mindcircles.co.uk.

Qvolution for individuals provides the questionnaire with results and also access to the web-enabled program which is based around the '7 Attributes for Success' techniques but has many more strategies for dealing with life.


## 4.2 WHAT IS STRESS?

The topic of stress is not finite. It does not end. We don't suddenly read or use a strategy and we are 'cured' from being stressed. Using any technique is a long term process and the techniques need to be repeated (yes – my systematic repletion (go back and read about this again if you need to remind yourself what that is).

It is very important to realise that help is at hand in the form of tips, tools, strategies, techniques, call them what you like and if you systematically repeat them it will improve your life. You will feel the benefit and be less stressed and can even prevent being stressed.

You need to know and understand the two types of stress, constructive and destructive.

Constructive stress is good for you. You need a certain amount of this kind of stress. You can enjoy the adrenalin boost.

The destructive stress is a known factor, according to research, in 70% of diseases. This is the unmanaged stress which not only destroys your productivity but also destroys your health.

Feeling stressed does not mean that you are neurotic. It is a perfectly natural response to events that threaten your safety. For example, at the first sign of danger, your whole metabolism switches on to a 'war' footing. You stop digesting food or making internal repairs. Your body is flooded with adrenaline and other emergency hormones to rush oxygen around your body and release quick energy fuel into your bloodstream. For a few minutes you are the strongest and fastest you can possibly be, just long enough to spear that wolf or run away from that landslide.

The stress response was designed for a time when danger was deadly but brief. However it is just as good today for the record-breaking leap to stop a child pulling a hot pan down on themselves or from running into a busy road into the traffic.

You will also experience the heart-thudding rush of stress when you are faced with a bill which you cannot pay or stuck in traffic when trying to get to an appointment on time.

Nowadays problems tend to be long term. Everyone wants some control over their lives and you are no different. The difficulties you face are that life is changing all around you and faster than ever before. You can be swept along with the tide. Jobs are insecure, marriage seems no longer to be a lifelong commitment, your food and environment are increasingly polluted, you work longer hours than ever and yet it is harder to make ends meet. The world seems to be full of danger to your children, relationships and family problems add to your list of worries, you feel responsible for everyone's well-being yet seem powerless to make everything all right all of the time. This is a recipe for destructive stress.

Don't worry my techniques and strategies are at hand. But you do need to work at them and use the systematic repetition method.

You have already read about my ABC core techniques but before looking at each of the attributes you need to consider what makes you stressed. These are called stressors.


### 4.3 STRESSORS

Stressors are situations or events which cause you to feel tense or stressed (strained). There are various categories and once again you can find more information on the worldwide web. However in this section I provide information on some of the categories.

**Frustration**: this can cause you to get stressed. Frustration occurs when you are unable to meet your needs or you are stopped from reaching a goal because of obstacles or when there is no ultimate goal in your mind. When you get frustrated you can get feelings of low self-esteem and worth.

You can get frustrated by your circumstances or surroundings (environment). Such circumstances are ones of prejudice, bias, unfulfilling job, death of a close friend or loved one. You can also get frustrated because of how you perceive yourself. This is internal frustration and includes perceiving yourself as lacking in worth, or feeling that you are not likeable. You have these perceptions because of your past conditioning. This is looked at in more detail in chapter 5.

**Conflicting situations:** this can cause stress. Such situations can be internal or external. The latter refers to arguments with colleagues, families, partners and so on. Internal conflicts arise when you are unable to choose between two or more options and even when you choose one option you get stressed because you perceive it to be the wrong choice or you are restricted by the choice you have made. When you are making a decision your cognition (thinking) and emotions are strained.

**Pressures:** these can also be internal or external. Pressures can cause you to be stressed and include changes at work or the need for you to work harder or faster or change direction to achieve a goal. You may have experienced pressure from your parents to do well at school or university or even be pushed to go to university. Again past conditioning affects you. You may stress yourself by putting pressures on yourself by failing to manage your time or fail to take time to relax, always work, work, work.

Of course none of the above are stand alone. They can be and are often inter-linked. Once you identify a stressor you assess it based on your personality, your emotions, your past experiences, your self-esteem, your past conditioning and your biological pre-disposition.

**Exercise:** take a few moments to think of what stresses you. Make some notes in the space below or just some mental notes. It is good to write them down as you can reflect on them later.

When faced with a stressful situation your physiology kicks in. Your central nervous system sends messages round your body telling it to prepare for 'fight or flight'.

## Fight or flight

The choice of 'fight or flight' will depend on how you assessed the stressor as either threatening or challenging. Physical changes start to occur in your body, such as the release of adrenaline and fatty acids, your heart rate and blood pressure increase. All this activity means that you are fully prepared for action. However nowadays you would not usually physically fight or run away from the stressor so everything that has been building up in your body is left there as residues. These residues cause you to remain feeling stressed. This is when you need to use techniques and strategies for de-stressing. My ABC core techniques are ideal for this. Later on you look at each of the attributes and will find more techniques for dealing with life in general.

**Exercise:** at this moment if you are feeling stressed, an excellent technique is to laugh or find something to laugh about! Remember laughter is your best medicine.

Having considered what stress is and some stressors that cause you to be stressed you need to look at the impact it has on you and those around you. In the next section I discuss symptoms of stress.

Certain life events have been researched[32] and shown to be stressful for individuals. According to Holmes and Rahe the top ten of these stressors are:-

Death of a spouse
Divorce
Separation from your spouse or partner
Imprisonment
Death of a close relative
Injury or illness
Marriage
Fired from your job
Reconciliation of spouses
Retirement

**Exercise:** look at the above list and tick what situation or situations you have been through. Then try out the full Holmes-Rahe Stress Inventory in Appendix I.

**(Notes)**

---

32  Holmes-Rahe *Social Readjustment Rating Scale*, Journal of Psychosomatic Research, Vol II, 1967

## 4.4 Impact of Stress (symptoms)

In the previous section you read some information about 'what is stress' and some of the stressors that cause you to be stressed.

Stress is different for every individual. No two individuals will experience stress in the same way or even in similar situations or circumstances. However destructive stress impacts on everyone. Below you read about some of the symptoms of stress and how it can impact on your life.

Stress has a very definite effect on your wellness and the degree of stress experienced will influence how much of an effect there is on you.

Stress is often accompanied by an array of physical reactions. These symptoms can be characteristic of other physical or mental disorders.

I was involved along with my good friend and colleague Chris Gibbons[33] in a television program on stress in teachers[34]. Chris is also an expert on stress in the nursing profession.

My experience of stress and my research focuses on health and safety legislation in relation to stress and as I said previously I am eager to show people how they can manage and even prevent stress. Therefore, it is important to understand the impact of stress and the symptoms. Understanding stress in the workplace is important too as research shows that in Europe, there is a major increase in depression, breakdown of families and communities and a constant sense of pressure of time and money. Organisations contribute to this by creating anger and anxiety instead of optimism and confidence among employees.[35]

---

33  Dr Chris Gibbons, Queens University, Belfast, School of Nursing
34  Teachers TV ( 2007) Stress Project at Kings Langley School, Herts
35  *The human workforce: People Management, teamwork and effectiveness in organisations,* West, Michael, Journal of International Business Studies, 2008

The specific signs and symptoms of stress vary widely from individual to individual and can be experienced as physical symptoms or cognitive, emotional, behavioural or all four. Some symptoms in the various categories are listed below.

- Physical symptoms include headaches and muscle tension.
- Cognitive symptoms include problems with your memory.
- Emotional symptoms can be moodiness and irritability.
- Behavioural symptoms include eating more or eating less.

For a full list of symptoms in each of the areas go to Appendix I.

Stress is a complex topic and in order to manage and even prevent stress in your life you need to learn how to recognise stress in yourself. As you now know from reading the above information stress affects your mind, body and behaviour in many ways and it is all directly tied to the physiological changes of the 'fight or flight' response.

If you begin by knowing what stresses you then you can take early steps to deal with any stressful situation before it spirals out of control. Chapter 2 provides you with my ABC core techniques to help you de-stress, manage and even prevent stress towards improved overall well-being. Some of the benefits of the techniques include reduced, stress, increased energy, raised morale, increased self-esteem and confidence and easier handling of difficult situations and challenges.

**Exercise:** before going on to read about each of the 7 Attributes reflect on what you have read so far and think of a difficult situation or person, maybe write down how you feel, what you have done in the past and then think again and try out one or all of my ABC core techniques.

(Notes)




**Exercise:** before moving on, finish with a short positive affirmation just for you. Something such as 'I feel good' or 'I feel positive' or make up your own! Write this down in the space below.

(Notes)




Read on and enjoy.

CHAPTER 5

# Attribute 1 – Self-awareness

*You never know yourself till you know more
than your body.* Thomas Traherne

To make the most of your life and take a step towards a
better way of being you need to learn how to become self-aware.
So what is self-awareness and how can you learn to become self
aware?

## 5.1 WHAT IS SELF-AWARENESS

*Knowing others is wisdom, knowing
yourself is Enlightenment.* Tao Tzu

Self-awareness is finding out who you are and what your
strengths and weaknesses are.

It is the first step towards a better way of being. As your self-
awareness grows you will start to understand why you feel the
way you do, what you feel and why you behave as you do.

Once you understand these things it gives you the opportunity and freedom to change those things you would like to change about yourself and thereby create the kind of life you want for yourself.

Without understanding and being aware of who you are you cannot change things. When you are clear about who you are, you can start to look at what you want and why you want it. This empowers you to make changes and choices.

You also need to challenge past conditioning and beliefs but before that you first need to learn about yourself or you will continue to get caught up in unknown beliefs and allow unknown thought processes to determine your feelings and actions. This is like going through life with the mind of a 'stranger'.

If you are going to move successfully forward to a better life self-awareness is one of the most important attributes to have and underpins all the others.

Now you might be saying to yourself at this stage that you know who you are and are perfectly self-aware. Don't be fooled. It is not an easy attribute to understand and may even be confused with self-consciousness.

So let's start with a definition of both self-awareness and self-consciousness.. There may be other definitions but for now a short one for each will suffice.

Self-awareness is the understanding that you exist as an individual with your own private thoughts. Self-awareness is a unique type of consciousness in that it is not always present.

On the other hand you probably understand the meaning of self-consciousness as being when you are worried about how you appear to others, that is, when you are self-conscious you can feel too aware of your actions and it can impair your ability to perform. Think of a concert pianist or singer, if they are self-conscious their hands may become stiff or throat restricted and worse still they may lose the ability to perform when they notice the audience. However in the context of this chapter the meaning of self-consciousness is about the development of your identity. It is about knowing yourself objectively and this plays a big part in how you behave. It affects people in different ways and different cultures vary in the importance they place on self-consciousness.

Self-awareness and self-consciousness are linked. John Locke[36] was very interested in human understanding and according to him personal identity (the 'self') depends on consciousness. You are the same person to the extent that you are conscious of your past and future thoughts and actions just as you are of your present thoughts and actions.

> *Our business here is not to know all things, but those which concern our conduct. If we can find out those measures... we need not to be troubled that some other things escape our knowledge.* John Locke

So how can you become self-aware? Where is it processed? Research by Ilan Goldberg[37] through an MRI experiment showed that self-awareness appears to be processed in the superior frontal gyrus (this makes up about one third of the frontal lobe of the human brain, one of the prominent bumps on the surface of your brain!).

There is also a link between self-awareness, self-consciousness and self-esteem. Most people will have suffered from self-consciousness at some point in their lives. You can probably recall a time when you were self-conscious and how it affected you. Not only did it affect your self-esteem but also your confidence. Past conditioning also affects your awareness such as. Think about how you have been brought up. Were you told not to boast about yourself, after all, no-one likes a big-head? Or were you told .you had a big ego? Ego is discussed later on in section 5.3.

With all these links between self-awareness, self-consciousness, self-esteem, confidence and ego you are probably feeling confused and wondering what it is all about. Briefly:

---

36  Locke, John (1689) *On Identity and Diversity* in an Essay Concerning Human Understanding

37  Goldberg, Ilan (2006) *A functional magnetic resonance imaging*

- You need to be self-aware but not so much that you become too self-conscious
- You don't want to be too self-conscious because this affects your self-esteem
- If too self-conscious it knocks your confidence
- You don't want to be so over confident that you come across as arrogant and big-headed
- If you are big-headed then you are thinking of your ego instead of your self-esteem
- And so on and so on......

More Confused? Don't worry. You are going to read about all these areas and have tips and tools to use to keep you feeling good about yourself.

**How do you become self-aware then maintain your self-awareness?**

In order to make the best of your self-awareness attribute you need to examine your belief system. This may sound easy but you may not want to do this because it means being prepared to face the truth about yourself and this could in all probability be painful.

It is also more than likely that when you know who you are you may have to change! Lots of people just do not want to do this because they are afraid and it takes effort!

In short, self-awareness requires honesty and courage. You will learn more about courage in Chapter 7 which is about 'audacity' the third attribute.

Everyone has strengths and weaknesses, qualities and flaws. If you are anything like me you may often think you have more flaws than qualities! After all you don't want to be thought of as boastful and big-headed. So how do you find out who you really are? You need to look at your past conditioning and your belief system. Were you encouraged to do things, encouraged when you did well or praised (more on the difference later), or were you told not to boast, not to talk about yourself.

You need to trace your thoughts and behaviour back to the beliefs you have. You will see a logical progression to the steps you take when faced with different situations, people and life itself. You need to identify your underlying beliefs. Are they your beliefs or those of someone-else whether your parents, authority figures in your life, your peers and so on.

## Challenging your belief system

Before challenging your belief system please be assured that it is ok to be where you are 'at' in life and you must remember that most people do the best they can at any point in time based on their current belief system and with all the information they have at that time.

It is difficult to understand this because often you may not think of it as having been your best.

How many times have you said to yourself '*if only I could do that over again I would have done it differently*'? but how many times do you try to find out the reason why you acted that way and not another way? Despite asking the 'if only' question do you ever analyse your reasons. Probably not, but there are reasons and you would find out these reasons if you took time to trace back your thoughts and behaviour to your beliefs.

Already you may be thinking this is far too complex and time consuming to do. The good news is that, for now, it is ok to BE who you are. The best news is that you are going to KNOW who you are!! This includes your strengths and your flaws or weaknesses. I prefer to call weaknesses your challenges because it seems a more positive, forward thinking word and I have found that it is through your challenges that you will find your greatest strengths.

A belief is an idea which you consider to be true. What you have to look at now is whether the beliefs you hold now are yours or someone-else's, such as your parent, authority figures who have influenced you as you grow up and this includes your colleagues, friends or peers.

You may have come to believe something about yourself which is totally untrue. This can come about through the labels that have been put on you as you grew up. I don't really like being labelled or using labels on other people but this exercise helps you to understand how you see yourself. Try the exercise below.

**Labels**

Imagine that you are describing yourself to a stranger (use only a few words). Be as honest as possible (no-one else need see or read this). What would you say? How would you 'label' yourself?

What did you write? Did you describe your job, your hobby or did you say you are a mum, a housewife, a sister, a husband, a brother and so on.

Worse still did you say that you are 'just' a housewife' or 'just' a typist. People do tend to play down what they do and who they are for fear of being thought of as big-headed and arrogant. This is because you have been conditioned in the past by your parents or authority figures not to talk about yourself, told not to be selfish, told not to boast, told to think of others before yourself and so on. A bit like the phrase children should be seen and not heard.

So is there a correct answer? Well to help you towards self-awareness you have to start by asking yourself the same question and answering (quietly and in your head) 'I AM ME'. I suppose this is a kind of label too.

**LABELS!** These are given to you early on, even just after you are born. He has his dad's eyes. She has her mother's nose. Isn't he small? Isn't she big? Perhaps you were the second born and someone says 'Oh what a lovely wee brother for Jean......' Do you resonate with this? Are you always Jean's wee brother, or John's wife, or the secretary, the general dogs body???

Most people mean well but even positive labels can have negative effects. For example perhaps you have been labelled by your family as the 'clever one'., always hearing your brother and sister being told by family and teachers 'why can't you be as clever as your brother/sister ......' you recognise this as being negative for your sibling but equally, although appearing to be a positive label for you, it can have negative effects because even when you just want to be 'you' , maybe act frivolously or silly, you feel as if you have to live up to this 'cleverness' all the time! Whether the negative or positive label, all anyone really wants to do is scream 'I AM ME'.

Until you are aware of who you are, you cannot possibly try to identify who or what someone else is.

To help you remain positive throughout the process of change a quick effective way is by using the ABC core techniques but particularly the A for affirmation. Your physiology takes only a matter of seconds to change from feeling 'low' to 'happy' and surely you would want to feel happy. Affirmations can do this and the good news is that you do not have to believe what you are saying, just by saying it helps. Affirmations along with creative imagery makes you feel good and can help you achieve goals. Athletes do this.

You should now be getting the hang of who you are and if you use the ABC core techniques you will start to feel better about yourself. You will also find that you start looking at yourself before 'blaming' others.

Self-awareness is a major attribute and underpins all the others. However it is or may be early days for you in this learning curve. Don't be anxious, remain positive.

You may be the kind of person who is wary of taking risks and frightened of changes of any kind. My intention is that with effective techniques you can do and be the best you can be.

Successful risk takers carefully calculate the risks. Those who plunge in without thinking of themselves or others are heading for disaster. It does not mean that we never plunge in – there are times when this fits the situation. It might be in a crisis.

Life is funny in this way. When we are thrown into some traumatic situations some people have the ability to know instinctively what to do and wade in without thought for themselves. These are the heroes and of these there are many. This does not mean that you are any less a person just that you are different as we all are. It would be an odd world indeed if we were all the same.

So how do you become the most successful person you can be, for YOU. You can do this by looking at your **paradigm**. This is just a fancy word for your 'pattern'.

Your 'pattern' over the years has been changed, altered, enhanced even distorted by the labels you have been given by others or even given by yourself.

## 5.2 HOW TO FIND OUT WHO YOU ARE

You need to start by looking inside yourself and finding out what your strengths and weaknesses are. This is a difficult thing to do because you may not like what you discover.

However remember that you are reading this book in private. Everything is for 'your eyes only' (unless you want to share the information). So you can and must be honest with yourself. If you are not honest with yourself then the only person you are hurting is YOU.

*Be true to yourself.* Anon.

Once you know what your strengths and weaknesses are you can work to diminish your weaknesses and work on your strengths.

When you focus on improving your strengths then you can find your true potential. You can also pull on your strengths no matter what difficult situation or person you face. This can improve your overall well-being, make you feel good about yourself and those around you.

*You are what you are and where you are because of what has gone into your mind. You can change what you are and where you are by changing what goes into your mind.* Zig Ziglar

## Using Questions To Become Self-aware

One technique to find out who you are and become self-aware is to ask yourself questions.

*Let us not look back in anger, nor forward in fear, but around in awareness.* James Thurber

Questions can help you become more self-aware. Are you where you live? Are you your job? Are you what you look like? The answers to these questions are only reflections of who you are to the outside world. But it's just that, a reflection of your inner self. To go below the surface you need to ask yourself what type of people do you enjoy spending time with. The answer to this should be open-minded people because you can explore more ideas with them and enjoy searching for answers. More than this, open-minded people will not make fun of you or your ideas. Why would you want to be with people who make you feel bad or horrible? You want to be with people who accept you the way you are. However you may be someone who enjoys making fun of others.

There are many assessment and profiling tools and instruments used usually in the workplace scenario.

When used in the workplace you can and may get upset by the answers they throw up and worse than that you may perceive that they are shared with lots of others (whether they are or not). However you still need a starting point for your questions. I use five ordinary everyday shapes. There has been research on shapes but I use them in a different way.

The five shapes can be found in Appendix III. Your starting point is to choose two shapes. Do NOT think about them just look and choose the two that you like best. Remember this is for your eyes only. You are not going to be analysed.

Once you have looked at the shapes in Appendix III write down the two shapes that you liked the best.

Now read about the strengths and weaknesses that relate to your choice. If you don't like what you read you might want to choose again but you will soon realise that each of the shapes carries strengths and weaknesses. This is intended as a guideline only to help you ask yourself questions.

I can share with you that my choices are squiggle and circle. Read about 'who I am'. I have to work at focusing on my strengths! It is hard work and you will probably find the same but really worthwhile.

The strengths and weaknesses are only a brief guideline, a starting point for you. Please treat it so and start to ask yourself what strengths and weaknesses you have.

## CIRCLE

**General Strengths (tendency/sometimes):** friendly, good natured, person-oriented, enjoy working with people, respect others, sensitive, flexible and open to change, non-confrontational.

**General weaknesses/challenges (tendency/sometimes):** stretch yourself too think, think more about others than yourself, too talkative, learn to enjoy your own company, make time for yourself, too trusting.

## SQUIGGLE

**General Strengths (tendency/sometimes):** creative, visionary, open to all ideas, imaginative and curious, non-confrontational, untraditional, see the bigger picture for yourself and others.

**General weaknesses/challenges (tendency/sometimes):** a dreamer, often fantasise, removed from reality, appearing to see the bigger picture but often fixed on your own ideas and creativity and closed to others, even dis-interested.

## SQUARE

**General Strengths (tendency/sometimes):** a planner, organised, clear focus and direction, self-satisfied, relaxed and calm, down to earth, friendly and helpful, comfortable with yourself, self-assured and secure, traditional and conformist.

**General weaknesses/challenges (tendency/sometimes):** rigid, often obsessive list maker, require direction and clear instruction, insecure and nervous, worrier with fears of unknown, difficulty in delegating, closed to other ideas, can appear selfish and controlling, skeptical, like own space.

## TRIANGLE

**General Strengths (tendency/sometimes):** organized, reliable, dependable, hard working, assertive, self-disciplined, eye for detail, meticulous, punctual, focused, confident, goal oriented, seek productivity and profitability, seek equality in work and social relationships.

**General weaknesses/challenges (tendency/sometimes):** money oriented, selfish and aggressive, working to rules but blocked when too focused or closed, up tight, controlling and manipulative.

# RECTANGLE

**General Strengths (tendency/sometimes):** good natured, helpful and forgiving, attention to detail, organised but flexible, good adviser and counselor, ability to listen to others and other ideas, stable, patient and kind, friendly manner.

**General weaknesses/challenges (tendency/sometimes):** gullible and insecure, quite rigid and sometimes impatient, lack confidence cynical, need direction, uncomfortable and introverted.

The shapes exercise is not a trivial one and should not be used lightly. Although sometimes they are used as an ice-breaker this is by a professional facilitator to avoid the upset that labeling can cause particularly in an open forum. Remember this exercise is for your eyes only and the true purpose here is for you to find out who YOU are and not label others. It is recommended that you do this when you are reading alone and have time to think about what the exercise and shapes mean.

## 5.3 DIFFERENCE BETWEEN SELF-ESTEEM AND EGO

Another important point when finding out 'who you are' is not to let your strengths 'go to your head' and ignore your weaknesses. If you think that you only have strengths ask yourself if you are being honest with yourself. Are you being true to yourself? Make sure you are not being big-headed or full of ego. It is ok to recognise your strengths and be confident and have self-esteem. It is not ok to be boastful and full of yourself.

Self-esteem often gets confused with ego! Self-esteem means having a proper estimation of your inner self. It has nothing to do with ego. People with high self-esteem are good to have around you because they try new things and new adventures. They also increase the self- esteem of others. You should try to develop this in yourself, then your family, friends and even your community.

Self-esteem starts on the inside - in your mind and in everyone's mind. A good affirmation for building self-esteem is to remember that only the best is good enough for you. Repeat it and write it down.

**Exercise:** write down the following affirmation and say it three times in your head, or aloud if you are alone or better still write it down three times.

*Only the best is good enough for me*

There are many definitions of ego, self-esteem and self-image some even by experts. I believe some are flawed such those who believe bullies have low self-esteem. If you consider the way bullies behave they have a narcissistic view of themselves and I would call this ego-esteem. So it is important to clarify what I believe to be the key definitions.

Self-esteem is how you feel about your inner self, your inner qualities. It is how you feel about your worth as a human being as you judge it.

Self-image is how you think you appear to others on the outside. This includes whether you think you are popular or pretty or smart, based on other people's judgment.

Ego-esteem is thinking that you are better than others. You feel important by making others feel unimportant. You are self-centred and egotistical.

Now take a moment to think about the definitions above and someone who is a bully (even yourself!). You will realise that the bully does not feel like a worthwhile human being. The bully builds themselves up by tearing others down.

While focusing on your strengths you can also build your self-esteem and that of others around you, such as children, family, friends and colleagues. You can do this by using encouragement which does not label. Encouragement is the fifth attribute and is discussed in more detail in chapter 9. However some information on the difference between encouragement and praise is given here.

If you praise someone you might use the words you make me happy, you did a good job, I'm proud of you and so on. However when you say these phrases you are judging whether the person receiving the praise is worthy of these words. So you only get praise for doing a good job if you actually do a good job. This builds self-image but it can also lead to building ego-esteem as it does not address any negative aspects of performance. It does not address inappropriate behaviour.

On the other hand encouragement builds self-esteem. It differs from praise in that it uses descriptive words and this increases internal motivation. For example you can tell someone that they really helped the family or team colleagues by doing that job and asking them how they feel about what they did. If a child does something around the house don't just praise them but say something such as 'I bet you feel proud of yourself'.

Encouragement of this type allows the person receiving the encouragement to judge their own work. It provides guidelines for setting standards and self-evaluating their work in the future. Even if someone does not do a perfect job you can still encourage them by asking what they might do next time or if they don't know, tell them that you will show them.

Take a moment to think about the type of praise (or lack of encouragement) in your workplace or home or among friends. Having read about the difference between praise and encouragement you should now be aware and know what to do to improve life around you.

Focus on the internal qualities and the positive aspects of what was done then decide whether it is necessary to point out any shortcomings. If you encourage people (and yourself) you and others are more willing to notice areas that need improving.


## 5.4 Past Conditioning

*Far too many people have no idea of what they can do because all they have been told is what they can't do. They don't know what they want because they don't know what's available for them.* Zig Ziglar

You have already read a definition of self-image. Indeed the concept of 'Self-image' is a major theory in psychology. According to this theory you are what you are because of the way you see yourself. You also have many self-images. What are your self-images? Write some down. These might include you as:

- a parent
- a son or daughter
- an employee
- a friend
- a sister/brother
- a golfer
- and more

What is happening here is that you are giving yourself labels or other people are giving you labels.

These self-images/labels can and often do control your behaviour and make you the parents, friends, sons, employees, golfer, etc. that you are. You act and live according to your self-images. It is important that you seek to find out your true self and the quality of your true self. You have been doing some of this when reading about self-awareness but ask yourself if this is the 'real' you, the 'true' you. So what if it is not the real you. How can you change this? You can do this by examining, reviewing and challenging your belief system.

### 5.5 CHALLENGING YOUR BELIEFS AND PAST CONDITIONING

*The greatest discovery........ is that a human being can alter his/her life by altering his/her attitude'*
**William James, American Psychologist**

You can start this process by asking yourself some questions.

- What beliefs do you have that hold you back?
- Are these really your beliefs or those of others who have told you?
- What conditioning is stopping you from moving forward in life?

These questions are about the way you think. Your thoughts determine your actions.

*Change the way you think and you change
the way you act and the way you are*

The quality and quantity of your beliefs determine how you work and act and how your life goes on from day to day.

Once you lock on to an opinion, belief or attitude about yourself you may or will find it very difficult to see or understand new truths about yourself and your environment.

Consider again the labels you have been given by others or labels you have given yourself. Did someone ever tell you that you were lazy? ugly? or that you could not do sums?

It might even have been a positive label such as being told you are 'the cleverest'? Even a positive label can be upsetting or destructive as it can place pressure on you to live up to the expectations of that label.

Labelling holds you back. To grow and develop you need to reflect on whether or not you are attached to anything such as:

- People
- Prejudices
- Life styles
- Work habits

that prevent you from seeing options for growth and development.

This does not mean that you have to give up old friends or holiday places. The labels are only negative if they are holding you back from accomplishing your goals/visions/dreams or if you hang on to them believing that they are what bring you happiness.

Locking on to an opinion, belief or attitude is not always bad. If you lock on to something positive, this is good. It helps you focus on the challenge and lock out distractions. High performance people lock on in constructive ways.

You can challenge your beliefs by asking yourself some questions. Has anyone ever said to you 'Better safe than sorry'? This kind of belief actually holds you back. It is a barrier to progress. However many people are afraid of failure and afraid of change (better the devil you know...) even if the change is positive and beneficial.

Some people prefer to play it safe in both personal and professional lives. If you want to lead a successful to and positive life you must overcome the beliefs that hold you back even though there will be risks. Any change requires moving away from the familiar. Any learning experience carries with it the risk of losing face. No wonder people stay where they are!

A fear that started when you were not even old enough to understand the process eventually impacts on your beliefs as an adult. Sometimes you may not know that you have been conditioned. Think of or write down one or two beliefs that you hold. Think about them and then ask yourself if these beliefs are your beliefs or those of someone else. Are these beliefs based on your experience or that of someone else? Have any of these beliefs ever been challenged by your reality or your own experience? Have these beliefs ever kept you from achieving a goal? If they are preventing you from achieving your goals are you willing to change one or more of them?

Some things you might have written down will include perhaps what football team you support, is this your family's team or yours. Or the political party you support, is this your choice or your family's? Are you in an unhappy marriage but believe that you cannot divorce because you have been conditioned (brought up) to believe that it is wrong to divorce?

So you see it can be a belief about anything, big or small but it affects your life. Start thinking about these beliefs and whether they are your beliefs. From childhood to adulthood you have been influenced by parents, teachers, authority figures in such ways that the political views, religious views and more that you hold are not actually yours but have come from your family or other authority figures.

Start thinking about these views and beliefs now, they may actually be your views but there is no harm in challenging them particularly if they are holding you back from achieving your dreams. Then make up your own mind. At least if you have done this and they still hold you back you have only yourself to look to!

By reflecting on and critically examining the belief system that you hold can help you develop and grow.

What belief system you hold is linked to your attitudes and behaviours. With all this knowledge you can open up your awareness and release your potential. You have the right to be and to function as you choose provided of course it does not hurt you or anyone else physically, mentally or emotionally. You can recognise that you have choices even though some of these choices may be painful.

**Fear of success**

I must say a few words about fear of success. Sounds silly doesn't it? However I believe this is what I suffered from in delaying the writing of this book.

I looked back at how long it has taken me to write this book, despite many people asking for it. Various thoughts went through my head from 'no-one will want to read it', 'there are many other books on well-being' to 'what if' it does so well I can't meet demand or by mentioning Qvolution what if the web-enabled program is not as perfect as I would like or people might be negative. Does this sound familiar to some of you? I believe this is 'fear of success', worries about not meeting or fulfilling expectations.

I also recalled someone at university who never sat his exams. When I asked him why, he told me if he did not sit them then he could not fail. Of course he left university without any qualifications but in his mind he had not 'failed'. This is sad because if you never try you will never know.

*If you never try you'll never know....*

So I sat down and reflected on 'why should I write this book'. I realised that I had been talking about the '7 Attributes for Success' for many years and despite being asked for the book I had not acted.

I had to use all 7 attributes to push beyond my fears and write the book. So here it is.

### 5.6 CHOICES

How do you see yourself in the future and where would you like to be. Would you like to be a valuable, interesting person, loving, kind, loyal and compassionate or do you want to feel unworthy, under-valued, lazy, mean and disloyal? I am sure you would rather feel valued and live life feeling good about yourself.

Surely everyone wants to feel good. You may not know it but you do have a wide range of choices but these may be painful and often people are afraid of change.

Your decisions may create challenges. Some may make you feel less complete or less satisfied. Of course you could just continue the way you are or better still you could live your life as a continuing process of adventure and discovery.

If you stay sharp and alert it will mean that most (and even all) the choices you make will be good ones, ones which help you and do not hurt you or others.

You may now even be realising that you have been burying yourself in work or play and have been avoiding the adventure and mystery of what a new positive life could bring. You have been avoiding a new journey. Some people even take the easy way out of too much drinking or even drugs.

You should be considering taking your new route and also sharing your new journey and the spirit of the great adventure with those around you. You must look inward to find the place in yourself that feels at peace and to find out who you are. With confidence, belief, patience and humour you can find LIFE rather than just existence.

*Life is what happens when we are busy*
*making other plans.* John Lennon

Why not take responsibility and give life up as a possession and take it back as a miracle!

Many people do many things but often never find what it is that would help make sense of life. Life is like the weather. Have you ever noticed that during a ferocious storm there is often a rainbow and after the storm there is often the most wonderful sunset.

Like many you may not know that the power to change your life is within you. If you always look to life as being dependant on other people and other things then it is out of your control. The task is to find something inside yourself that cannot be taken away. The way to do this is to use the ABC core techniques. This may sound too easy, too simple but they do work when used.

Another excellent way to discover your inner self is to meditate or do yoga and other such exercises. Even going for a walk in the park surrounded by the wonder of nature can help.

Although the exercises may sound and be simple the actual journey towards finding your 'inner' power is a long slow one. However, every journey starts with the first 'small' step.

It is not just prisoners who are 'closed in'. Ordinary people are 'locked in' by fear, anxiety, desires and anger. Looking within yourself will change the course of your life forever. Small steps such as doing the ABC core techniques, meditation and similar exercises as well as large steps such as doing everything with kindness, humour, patience, courage and self-honesty will change your life forever.

*The 'big view' is not from the widest ocean or the highest mountain but from 'deep within yourself'.*

The creative imagery technique is most effective in the process of change. Imagine if you did not know how to use your arms. Think of people who have this challenge and how limiting it must be for them, yet some wonderful people push through the limitation and don't let it hold them back.

Lots of people live, breathe, walk and talk but most of the time many do not use a fraction of their inner power. Are you one of these people?

Are you out of balance? Do you view life like a mouse? It does not have to be this way. Wisdom, joy and peace come only from learning how to see the bigger picture.

## 5.7 DAILY ACTIVITIES TO HELP YOU MOVE FORWARD

Now you may be thinking that the very words 'daily activities' will involve lots of time taken up in studying and practicing. Wrong. This is not what is meant or intended. I realise how busy life is for everyone and that is why I promote my ABC core techniques. If you have tried them and are now using them regularly you will know that they can be done in a matter of a few minutes. You can make them longer or shorter to fit with your lifestyle. All that I ask is that you make them a positive habit. They will improve your overall well-being.

In this section you have learned about self-awareness and the importance of knowing yourself - strengths and weaknesses – but more importantly how to focus on enhancing your strengths and how the ABC core techniques can help build and increase your confidence and self-esteem. All this is linked to the next attribute, resilience.

Chapter 6

# Attribute 2 – Resilience

*Obstacles don't have to stop you. If you run into a wall, don't turn around and give up. Figure out how to climb it, go through it, or work around it.*
Michael Jordon, Professional basketball player

## 6.1 WHAT DOES RESILIENCE MEAN?

Resilience is about 'bouncing back' against adversity. It is about dealing with difficult events that you face throughout life. These might be major or minor and can be the death of a loved one, terrorist attacks, traumatic events or loss of your job or an illness.

No matter whether major or minor the event affects you and you need to be able to adapt over time to different events, life-changing ones, stress ones and more. So why do some people adapt better than others?

Those who adapt well are those with more than self-awareness, they have resilience too. This is an on-going process that requires taking a number of steps but also requires time and effort. Everything worthwhile takes effort on your part.

Don't worry if you are one of those people that find it difficult to adapt to life-changing events. You can learn to develop and use strategies that not only develop resilience but enhance and increase it.

Research shows that resilience is not something extra-ordinary it is quite ordinary and this is shown in the response by many people to traumatic events such as terrorist attacks and their efforts to rebuild their lives after such an event.

It is worthwhile knowing that having resilience does not mean that you do not experience difficulty and distress. If you have suffered major adversity in life or a trauma it is common and natural for you to suffer emotional pain and sadness. Even your road to resilience will involve considerable emotional distress.

I believe that some people have 'resilience' – I call this an attribute. However as it involves certain behavior, thoughts and actions, it can be learned and developed. It is a personal process and as we are all unique you can develop it but your way of developing it might be and probably will be different from others.

You are going to learn how to develop resilience or enhance it. Having resilience will help you to deal better with life's changes and adapt to adversity and events which impact on your life, such as trauma, tragedy, threats and significant forms of stress and even small changes.

Although being resilient is a personal process there are effective factors that contribute to developing and enhancing resilience. You will learn more about these factors in the next section.


## 6.2 How to bounce back from set backs

There are certain factors which help you to bounce back from adversity and any setbacks that life throws at you.

One of the most effective factors which help you to face adversity is having caring and supportive relationships within and outside the family. If you have caring and supportive people around then these can provide role models for you. They can encourage you and help boost your resilience.

Another step in the process of developing resilience is to be able to make realistic plans but use small steps.

*A journey of a thousand miles starts with one small step.* Chinese proverb

Having resilience and the ability to bounce back is also inextricably linked to self-awareness, that is, your view of yourself. You have already read about and hopefully learned how to be more self-aware and about how being positive is a great asset to improving your overall well-being. So it is with resilience.

Having a positive view of yourself and confidence in your strengths and abilities can enhance your resilience. You might want to go back and look at what you found out about yourself and what your strengths and weaknesses were. Try to re-enforce your strengths by affirming them. Do and repeat an affirmation that follows the 3Ps principle. Remember that is a statement which is positive, personal and present. It can be as simple as 'I am resilient' or 'I am positive' or 'I am confident'. Building your confidence is important on your journey for developing resilience.

**Exercise:** say the affirmation 'I am confident' three times out loud or if in public, say it in your head. Better still write it down.

Part of the process in becoming more resilient is also looking back at some past experiences. You cannot change the past but you can change how you view it and learn from it. Life is full of obstacles.

*For a long time it had seemed to me that life was about to begin – real life. But there was always some obstacle in the way. Something to be got through first, some*

*unfinished business, time still to be served, a debt to be
paid. Then life would begin. At last it dawned on me
that these obstacles were my life.* Fr. Alfred D'Souza

Look at some past experiences and ask yourself how you
dealt with those experiences. Answer some questions such as
what events made you most stressed? In what way did these events
affect you? Who did you look to for support? What did you learn
about yourself? What did you learn about your relationship with
those who were supportive? Did it help assisting someone else
who experienced a similar situation or event? Did you overcome
obstacles and how?

Remember there are no fixed answers to these questions.
When thinking about them also think about how you and others
communicate with each other. Communication is an important
factor for resilience. However many people communicate
everyday but many do not do so effectively. Later on there are
some tips on how to make your communication skills more
effective and how to problem solve. With increasing cultural
diversity you are probably more aware now that communication
differs from culture to culture so remember your way might not
be their way!

You also need to be as flexible as possible to be resilient.
Being flexible helps you to manage strong feelings and impulses.
Remember it is ok to experience strong emotions but you need
to realise when you need to 'avoid' these strong emotions in

order to continue functioning. If you are flexible you can move forward and take action to deal with problems and be able to meet the demands of everyday life. However you also know when to step back, rest and renew your energy. The ABC core techniques can help with this. These help you to be confident. So what you are hoping for is being able to 'hold on' to all the positive ways of dealing with challenges. This means you need tenacity!

## 6.3 HOW TO 'HOLD ON' TO POSITIVES (TENACITY)

I have faced many challenges in life but so have many people. I was often called 'pig-headed' or 'bloody minded' but I think this has stood me in good stead. If someone said that I could not do something I would try to prove them wrong. Now this is ok but you have to be realistic and what I learned most was that I should not take risks but should consider the whole picture before jumping in. This really means taking 'calculated' risks. Entrepreneurs are not risk adverse but those who are successful are those who consider all avenues and therefore the risks they do take are carefully thought out, not all the time of course and even the calculated risks may not turn out to be successful. One thing those people will have in common is that they will learn from their mistakes and their failures. Now this lesson is sometimes not learned first time round! For me in certain aspects of my life, it has been third or even fourth time round! So don't panic you are not alone.

Try to avoid the view that a crisis is insurmountable. Many events that are highly stressful are outside your control but what is in your control is the way you interpret and respond to them. Use the ABC core techniques to be more positive especially about how future circumstances may, and can, be better.

Learn to accept that change is part of living. Remember that you cannot control everything that happens to you but you can focus on the things that are within your power to change.

It is important to have dreams and have a vision of what you would like your life to be. Your vision is on-going and to make this happen you should set goals but these should be realistic. Doing something regularly helps you move towards achieving your goals. This is why the ABC core techniques are effective when used regularly.

Focus on something that you know you can achieve and that will help you accomplish your goal. Ask yourself what you can accomplish that could take you one step nearer your goal.

Don't fall into the trap of putting aside tasks or actions until later. I do this sometimes and despite thinking it would make you happy to leave a task that you don't want to do until later it does not. This is called procrastination and it is counterproductive, needless and delaying. Sometimes you might think that this will help you cope with anxiety. However it can result in stress or guilt and even a crisis. Does this ring a bell? Do you put things to the bottom of the pile, telling yourself you will do them later? It does with me but then it usually means a panic later when the task has to be carried out and usually less time to do it in!

So procrastinating means you are less productive and often causes disapproval in others for not meeting your responsibilities or commitments. However sometimes this results in you procrastinating even further.. Sounds and is a vicious circle!

Don't worry it is normal to procrastinate to a certain degree just not so much that it stops you from functioning normally.

I do procrastinate sometimes but I have learned how to tackle the problem by making a list of things to do.

Remember the 'square' – are you someone who makes lists about what you want to achieve each day? Well it's ok to do this but how do you feel when you do not achieve all the things on your list? Don't worry. What I do if I make a list is to make it as realistic as possible, taking account of the complexity or otherwise of the things to be done, the time in which they have to be done and then if I do not achieve everything that day I praise myself for what I have done and move on.

I do tend to procrastinate but I also know that I work well under pressure so if I need to get something done I set a 'time limit or deadline' for myself and try to keep to it. It doesn't always work but then that's life. If something gets in the way of my deadline I will review and see how I can adjust to make things happen and tell myself that 'the interruption' was supposed to happen and perhaps I had something to learn from it or should have been open to an opportunity that could have come from it.

Try to keep your eyes open for opportunities, keep an optimistic outlook as this helps you to expect that good things will happen to you. Use the creative imagery technique to imagine what you want, rather than worrying about what you fear. You might be someone who worries about things all the time, fretting over everything, thinking that the worst will happen. Do you know that worrying is just part of your imagination creating something that you don't want! If you find yourself worrying all the time, snap out of it immediately. Stop the 'what ifs' and use the positive affirmations to change your thoughts. They do work.

An excellent affirmation for this is saying to yourself 'only good things come to me'. Have you ever thought of something negative and it just seems to happen. This is called the law of attraction, that like draws like. So if this happens with negative things why not make it happen with something positive. Why would you want bad things to happen to you? I certainly only want good things to come to me. Just remember that worry creates more worry which creates even more worry!!

If you are having difficulty with something you should also try to enrol the help of positive supportive people. I have found this difficult as I believed I should know what I am doing or about my specialist subjects but any specialist subject is often so vast that we can't know everything. Also it might look as if I am a failure. However I learned that a very effective technique was to say that I did not know but I do know where to find the answer.

You will read later on about 'know how' the last attribute and learn that it is good to ask for help and information and gain knowledge.

When seeking help you should communicate effectively with other people. As I have already said we communicate everyday but much of this is not effective. Part of the difficulty is technology, such as, emailing, texting, messaging and more. Have you ever got annoyed at an email you received and think the person sending it is very abrupt? I know I have. Have you mis-interpreted a text? I know I have.

The most effective communication is still face-to-face because we communicate with our eyes, facial expression, body language, tone of voice and words. Research shows that the impact of a message is approximately 7% in the words, 38% vocal (that is tone and inflection) and 55% non-verbal (that is body language, facial expression, eyes). Some research indicates that the non-verbal can be as high as 65%. So you can see how emails and texting can easily be mis-interpreted.

For communication to be effective it must be between effective, responsible people. Issues I have encountered over the years has been in the areas of relationships counselling and business mediation or negotiation. Despite mediation being promoted as an effective way of resolving issues the difficulty arises when both or all parties are not open-minded, responsible and willing to effectively listen.

A problem sometimes arises in couples counselling when one party can speak eloquently and come across as a responsible, upstanding individual while the other party (often the woman) is reduced to a jibbering wreck perhaps rightly so as this is the partner that has been abusive (mentally, emotionally and/or physically) and she feels vulnerable when meeting face-to-face with this person, even with a third party (mediator) present.

I can share with you that I have personal experience of such a relationship and I recall not wanting to or being able to be in the same room as the other person even if a mediator were to be present.

In a mediation situation another problem that can arise is with the person who is the mediator. Even though there is training the personalities of all parties cannot be discounted and mediation may not be the answer or bring about the results hoped for by all parties. This topic of course is vast and worthy of a book on its own.

For everyday purposes you should try to communicate effectively as much as possible. I call such communication my effective listening model.

## MY EFFECTIVE LISTENING MODEL

This model results in effective communication. The model has four steps.

Step 1: The first step is to focus and attend. At this step you should be 'reading' the whole communication, words, tone, inflection, facial expression, eyes and body language.

Step 2: The second step is to acknowledge the other person. This does not mean you are accepting what they are saying but you show acknowledgement perhaps with a nod or 'mmh'.

Step 3: The third step is vitally important for effective communication. You should clarify any points that you did not understand or mis-understood. Again this is not accepting what the person is saying it is opening up the avenue for clear communication so that you do not mis-interpret.

Step 4: The fourth and final step is to respond. Most people mis-understand the word 'respond'. They believe that it means you are accepting what the other person is saying. This is not what 'respond' means. It might mean that you say you accept and agree but more often you might want to consider what has been said, reflect and give an answer later. This is exactly what you should say. You might even say 'I don't know' the answer or how to respond just now but I will go away and think about it and give you my answer later. This gives you and the other person time.

A vital aspect of team meetings or committees and similar is preparation. If you have been asked to a team meeting or committee where decisions are required to be made you follow the four steps above but prior to the meeting you should have undertaken preparation and sufficient research to listen and respond at the meeting.

However always remember that if you feel you cannot agree or decide you should communicate this and explain why. Perhaps you were not given sufficient time to research or another subject arose at the meeting that was different from the agenda and so on.

There are many different situations where you require to communicate and one of the most effective methods I have found is my effective listening model.

## Conscious choices

If you develop the ability to make conscious choices about your thoughts, feelings and behaviours regardless of circumstances or situations you can and will unlock your potential by realising you already have it.

*We cannot always control our thoughts, but we can control our words and repetition impresses the subconscious, and we are then master of the situation* Jane Fonda

Every effect has a cause. The situations and circumstances of our lives are the effects produced or caused by our actions. The first cause is our 'thought'. Close your eyes and focus on something good that has happened to you. This is using creative imagery. Very quickly (within about 30 seconds) chemicals are released that create a physical feeling of happiness. It is the same with sad or bad thoughts, chemicals are released that create a physical feeling of sadness. So why would you want to feel sad. Focus on the positive and you can create a physical feeling of happiness through this positive thought process. In addition to the creative imagery you can also use affirmations such as saying to yourself 'this is a good day'.

Everything starts as a thought, behavior starts as a thought, habit starts as a thought, emotion starts as a though. So remember your thoughts define your attitudes and influence your behavior.

*Health, happiness and success depend upon the fighting spirit of each person. The big thing is not what happens to us in life - but what we do about what happens to us.* George Allen

Linked to resilience is audacity. To be resilient requires the courage and strength to face your challenges. So what you do about what happens to you in life brings me to the next attribute – audacity. You read about audacity in the next section.

As with the other attributes I believe they are all inextricably linked. I believe many people have these attributes but not everyone uses or develops them. It is my hope that people will learn about themselves and what attributes they have and can develop. The qualities of courage and strength overlap and most of us would like to have these qualities and if you have children I am sure you would like your children to gain these qualities as part of their own character.

CHAPTER 7

# Attribute 3 – Audacity

*With audacity one can undertake anything, but
not do everything.* Napoleon Bonaparte

In the context of this book I look at audacity as having
courage and being brave, having the strength to not only face
life's challenges but push beyond them. In the words of Michael
Jordan:

*If you run into a wall, it is the ability to figure
out how to climb over it, through it or work
a way around it.* Michael Jordan

In times of much conflict the words courage, bravery and
strength increasingly appear in the media, newspapers and
television. For the purpose of this book I consider courage as the
ability to experience fear but continue to carry on in the face of
that fear and the ability to face challenging life experiences, keep
your composure and retain your 'strength' (forces) to carry on.

Do you consider yourself to be brave? Do you have courage
to face challenges or new situations and people or all that life

throws at you? How we behave and re-act is linked to our past conditioning. You may want to go back and look at that section again.

As children you may recall phrases 'be careful' or 'watch out' used by your parents. By saying these phrases your parents wanted to look after you, protect you. However sometimes it is these very phrases that 'hold you back' now from doing new things or meeting new people. What children really need is to be prepared for facing difficulties that life very likely will throw at them as they mature. If you are a parent you should try to help your child become independent and be able to face some adversity, within limits of course for their safety. Dependency, independency and inter-dependency are discussed later on in chapter 8.

Adversity is necessary to help develop composure to face the challenge and the courage and strength to overcome it and be successful.

If you are a parent with children or a carer of young people you should not try to 'coddle' them or over protect them to the point that they do not have a chance to gain courage and strength. Children need to develop strength and they can only do this if they make their own mistakes and learn from them and move on. If you want your children to be strong and courageous you need to have enough faith in their innate character that you let them grow. Encourage your child using phrases that reflect the 'feel good' factor for them.

If you recognise that you were over protected and held back then it's not too late. You can develop your 'audacity' by taking small steps to increase your strength and courage. You can do this by trying something new today. Even if it is small, like saying hello to a new colleague at work or to a new parent at the school you will start to gain strength and courage. While you are doing this use the ABC core techniques.

Remember also to encourage yourself it will make you feel good. Put yourself in situations where you have responsibility, some 'nerves' and are unsure. Go back to the section on stress. It is good to have some kind of stress, the constructive kind.

It is good for you to be nervous and unsure sometimes. You can overcome your nervousness and channel it. It prepares you for life and life can be hard. If you do this for a child or young person, courage and strength will be with them all their life. You too can start now to gain courage and strength to take you forward to a 'new' more positive life.

### 7.1 WHAT IT MEANS TO BE BRAVE

*Victory belongs to the most persevering.*
Napoleon Bonaparte

There are many stories of bravery, of heroes who have ignored their own personal safety to pull their colleagues to safety; of young children facing the trauma of a debilitating and sometimes terminal illness; of individuals saving others from fire, terrorist attacks and so on. These are our true heroes.

Those in the armed forces undergo training and are taught to act on command or instructions but even such training does not prepare these individuals for the actual event. Some instinctively know what to do and act as one would say 'on the spur of the moment'.

Indeed when asking some individuals who win awards for bravery how or why they acted the way they did often say they don't know. They say they were just doing their job or they were acting 'without thinking' because they saw others in danger.

Many children facing the challenge of a terminal illness are seen smiling and happy. Visit a children's ward in hospital and it is not a gloomy place. It is heart rendering but the positive atmosphere is essential to those with illness.

There is much research on laughter having a role in times of great challenges particularly those diagnosed with terminal illness. Unfortunately what happens when you hear that a loved one or close friend has been diagnosed with cancer is that you don't know what to say or do. Or you don't say anything in case you say the wrong thing. You pull away from the patient and yet it is the patient who desperately needs your attention.

So what can you do? Ask lots of people who have been in this situation, even the patients, and you will be told that families and close friends are a great source of comfort but so also is humour.

Humour is a great connector of people in tough times. Laughter is also your best medicine in times of illness. However people are still unsure what to do or say and the time has to be right for laughter. So it is up to the individual patient to set the tone and through laughter the person can teach their family and friends to connect with them.

### Laughter is the best medicine

I have had friends diagnosed with terminal cancer and what I admired most about one close friend in particular was not only how she faced the traumatic situation with strength and fortitude, undergoing lengthy and debilitating treatment but her positive attitude and humorous disposition. On one occasion when I attended the cancer clinic with her tea was being handed round by a laughing, smiling lady whom I thought was the 'tea lady' for the hospital. My friend put me right – she told me that this lady had been given only a few months to live. What an inspiration to others. Sadly my friend is no longer with me but I know she would approve of me telling this story. *So here's thinking of you Jenny.* I know you will be bringing joy to wherever you are now.

I believe and research shows that cancer and laughter do go hand in hand. But how can you accomplish this? It's not easy but remember you read earlier that if you cannot control a situation or the outcome then you have to let it go. Do this by changing your attitude towards it.

Now there are many patients who fall into deep depression when diagnosed with a serious or terminal illness. However there are many more who eventually realise that although they cannot change their situation they can change their attitude to the illness or situation.

Many do this by being positive and using the ABC core techniques but along with humour. I believe that humour is an essential ingredient in the recovery process and even if like my friend Jenny there is no recovery they have still remained positive and brought joy to many during their life. Jenny, like many, celebrated everyday as a gift. She did not allow her family members and close friends to live in fear that everyday might be her last. Jenny was the first to laugh and joke. She set the tone for family and friends and encouraged laughter and fun.

Another very close friend and colleague suffered a terrible accident with his grand-daughter who suffered terrible injuries which proved fatal despite some months in hospital. He has been and is a source of inspiration to me and all around. Although he has some terrible low times we are able to talk and have shared humour and laughter. Some people were horrified that we could laugh and share humour but he has told me that this has helped him through the dark times. Life does go on. You never forget but you can look at the good times you had with a loved one.

Even if you have not experienced any of these situations you will have experienced tough times. Laughter does really help.

Now be brave. Move out of your comfort zone even for a little while. This builds character and increases your confidence and self-esteem.

Have the audacity to face challenges and deal with life 'face on' means stepping out of your comfort zone. Why not try something you are not completely sure you can do. When did you last do this? It can be something quite small like smiling and saying hello to someone new or in the queue next to you at the supermarket or bank.

*Take time, make time everyday to love, learn, explore, care and live.* Patricia Elliot

## 7.2 Facing challenges

You now need to do an exercise!

**Exercise:** Take a few moments to think of a challenge you are facing and one that you feel you cannot overcome. Write down your feelings. Ask yourself why you think it is an impossible task.

Now write down the facts of the situation or circumstance and start to break it down into smaller parts. Is the outcome something you have control over and if so think of it as an opportunity to do something new, positive and even different.

If you have no control over the outcome then you need to let it go. Visualise the problem gone. Affirm that you are not affected by it. Why dwell on something you have no control to change or power to alter.

If you are one of those individuals who goes through life dwelling on the 'what if' or 'what might happen' then you are really missing out on living.

## 7.3 View challenges as opportunities

From now on you are going to look at challenges in a different way. If you can control the outcome or have power over the change then you can use a problem-solving approach, breaking down the situation into smaller parts, dissecting, examining and analysing.

If you have no control over the situation or outcome then let it go. Remember what I said about worrying and that it needs to stop. It is wasted energy It causes stress. Worry cannot change your circumstances or the situation, it only enhances it.

If you are having a challenging day or facing a particularly difficult challenge you can face it by changing your thoughts and way of viewing it. Life is challenging and if you change how you view it then you will move forward by thinking of the challenges as opportunities. Any difficult experience or test of your ability or demand on you is a challenge. You have learned about affirmations which are all about positive thinking.

Positive thinking is proven to be a very powerful psychological technique for improving your overall well-being. Opportunities are the chances you get in life to move forward but much of the time you may not even be aware of your opportunities.

Sometimes challenges are thrust upon us such as being made redundant. I have talked with many people over the years who have been made redundant and although this affected all these individuals the ones who made the most of it took it as an opportunity to do something else which in many cases proved to be better than their last employment. Many people are not satisfied with their work and yet when made redundant are upset and annoyed. Rather than seeing it as an opportunity for something new they remain victims and keep on asking 'why me'.

I am not suggesting that being made redundant is something good because it is more and more difficult to find employment in the financial climate of the day. However it is amazing how the power of positive thinking makes such a difference and those using this power have a better outlook on life and feel better about themselves. The confidence and esteem that was knocked out of them with the redundancy situation starts to return and they feel better about themselves. You too can learn to grow from challenging situations and strengthen yourself as a person.

You need to take a fresh look at things which come your way. Rather than having a negative outlook, think from a positive viewpoint and you will feel much better. You will be able to face up to whatever comes your way.

Take a moment to think of all the challenges that seem to keep coming to you, over and over again. Ask yourself why these challenges keep repeating themselves. You should start to realise that they come into your life for a reason. Shift your thinking and start seeing them as opportunities to learn and make positive changes in your life.

The same challenges used to come my way and I met the same kind of negative people, people who would drain me. Only when I realised that I was drawing these kind of situations and people to me did things change. I started to use the affirmations. One which is particularly effective for me (and many others) is to say to yourself that you deserve the best or 'only the best is good enough for me'. It does work. Try it. You will feel better and good things will start to happen.

*Only the best is good enough for me.*

CHAPTER 8

# Attribute 4 – De-attachment

*The only thing you will ever possess is yourself, and
that only briefly, if at all.* Rain Bojangles

From my conversations with many people and the talks I
have given over the years to varied audiences I can advise that
this is the most difficult attribute for people to understand. I am
going to try to do this in this section!

The simplest way to view de-attachment is to think of
attachment as possessiveness. Possessiveness leads to jealousy
and this is at the root of many broken relationships.

Now I am not talking about detaching yourself so that you
are so independent that you are remote from everyone and
everything. But you are not to be so dependent that you need
someone or something too much.

Have you ever said or heard someone say 'Oh I don't know
what I would do if he left me?' Worse still some people say 'I'd
die if she left me' and so on.

In this section you are going to learn about inter-dependence
which is more healthy and I call this my attribute of de-
attachment.

De-attachment is about identifying positive and negative feelings.

**Exercise** Choose a positive magical moment and re-live the moment. Write down your feelings.

This might seem a rather random exercise but it raises your self-awareness. Such moments are the results of your way of being.

Life is about relationships. We have family relationships, work relationships, friend relationships and even relationships with our pets. I read the other day that business is about relationships. At a recent meeting where people were sharing stories of their work and businesses all agreed that it is not the business plan or the strategy that makes a good business but the 'people' and if they are positive, self-confident and feel valued then the business will prosper.

So if your relationship is not working what do you do? Struggle on, leave it, separate......?

Now I am not suggesting that you get divorced or you leave work or drop your friends but I am suggesting and recommending that you address the problem. Burying your head in the sand is no answer whether this is home or work but doing something about it is also not easy no matter whether it is your marriage or your work.

**Exercise**

Write down the name of the person who is the most important person in your life.

This is not a trick question but you may be surprised by the answer.

Answer – you should have written your own name!

You may not have thought about writing your name because of past conditioning. Like me you may have been told, when growing up, that it is selfish to think of yourself first. However if you don't take care of yourself and are happy with yourself then you cannot do this for other people. Also it is false thinking to believe that someone else can make you happy. Only you can make you happy. If someone else makes you happy then that is a bonus.

If you are confident and happy then you will draw likeminded people around you. If you see yourself as a victim then you will draw people around you that will treat you this way. Once again you need to change your thinking.

So let's look at jealousy and possessiveness.

## 8.2 JEALOUSY AND POSSESSIVENESS

Are you a 'green-eyed monster'? Are you jealous and possessive? Does it affect your relationships whether with a spouse, partner or even your family and friends. You might be jealous if your friend meets up with another friend and has not invited you along. Does all this sound familiar? Have you ever said 'what's my husband doing talking to the new next door neighbour? I think he touched her arm?'

When you feel a surge of jealousy, particularly, sexual jealousy you are responding to the possibility that you might be abandoned by your partner. Some say it is all down to your genes and the basic strategy of guarding your mate. However this book is not the place for an in-depth discussion on genes. Jealousy is an emotion and usually refers to negative thoughts and feelings of insecurity, fear and anxiety over the anticipated loss of something that you value. You usually experience a combination of emotions such as anger, sadness and even disgust. Jealousy is a familiar experience in relationships. It is also the theme of many novels, songs, films and poems.

If you get jealous you need to identify whether your feelings are coming from your own insecurity and that there is no reason for you to be jealous or possessive. If this is the case then you need to realise that you cannot make someone else behave the way you want them to behave.

If you feel you have reason to be jealous and that there is something that has set this off then this is a warning sign that all is not well in the relationship. Jealousy is not an easy thing to get rid of or ignore. It can 'eat you up'. Jealousy can also arise if you feel insecure and have a poor sense of self. Your jealousy can also drive your partner away and into the arms of someone else – the very thing you don't want to happen.

What you have to understand is that guaranteed fidelity is not really attainable. You cannot be with someone twenty four hours a day, three hundred and sixty five days a year. Eternal commitment cannot be guaranteed.

If you have a passionate concern and respect for the relationship you have with someone else then this helps you to attend to their feelings without rage, criticism and despair. This is a rational approach to a relationship.

The destructive jealousy is the type that you need to avoid or try to avoid. This type of jealousy operates below your level of conscious awareness. You are jealous often without even being aware of what you are doing. You constantly demand reassurance that you will always be the first and only person in your partner's life and you would be destroyed as a person if you were rejected. However remember that perfect reassurance does not really exist and in any case you do not need this. You can use your energy to focus on improving your own confidence and self-esteem and improving your relationship with your partner and all those around you.

**Resisting Jealousy**

Jealousy arises when you feel insecure and lack confidence. When you feel jealousy arising remind yourself that you are a 'whole' person with or without your partner. Affirm that you want a good relationship and be open and honest with yourself and when communicating with your partner or others. Remember that communication should be effective. Go back and read again about how to communicate effectively.

Remind yourself that you can function independently as a human being. You do not need or want to be dependent on someone else for your happiness. Remember that jealousy is a measure of insecurity not love. Don't be fooled when someone tells you that they want to know where you are and who you are with because they love you. This is emotional manipulation and they are doing it not because they love you but because they are insecure. If there is jealousy in a relationship it is highlighting that there are problems in your relationship which you should face and address.

Jealousy can reach levels of more than just words but into rage and even violence. Remove yourself immediately from a violent situation. No-one should make you feel bad about yourself. No-one has the power to do this unless you let them do it.

Anger is a destructive emotion. Just because you unleash it does not mean that it goes or diminishes. It can cause you to feel mentally and even physically ill. Holding your anger in can also be damaging to your health but it should be released in an appropriate way – a simple technique can be to 'punch a pillow, or going to a place where you can be totally alone and even screaming, a few people tell me that they sing at the top of their voice. Many people exercise, run, jog or go to the gym. All these things are good but you should also work out your mind by doing the ABC core techniques.

If you react negatively to your partner you will just keep making the same mistakes over and over. By reacting negatively I mean responding defensively or even sulking and being moody.

To avoid feeling negative emotions rise and making negative responses learn to build your confidence and affirm that you are positive. You can also decide what kind of relationship you want with your partner by asking yourself if you want a relationship based on co-operation or do you want a partner who always does what you want. Is your anger helping you to be the person, parent or partner you most want to be? Is your emotional well-being and emotional well-being of those you love important to you? I am sure you would want to answer yes to these questions.

What these questions are asking you to focus on is being interdependent rather than dependent on another human being for your happiness.

### 8.3 DIFFERENCE BETWEEN INTERDEPENDENCE AND DEPENDENCE

For the purposes of this book interdependence is about being mutually and physically responsible to and sharing a common set of principles with others. Such relationships imply that the individuals are emotionally and morally interdependent and inter-connected.

*Interdependence is and ought to be as much the ideal of man as self-sufficiency. Man is a social being. Without interrelation with society he cannot realize his oneness with the universe or suppress his egotism. His social interdependence enables him to test his faith and to prove himself on the touchstone of reality.* Mahatma Gandhi

There are various stages of growth from when you are born through to adulthood. At birth and when very young you are dependent on others to take care of you. You are then told that you need to learn to be independent, make your own decisions and take care of yourself. You are probably told that successful people don't depend on others, they are independent and therefore you are encouraged to become independent.

However I believe and in reality we are interdependent. Life requires 'leaders' and 'teams'. However to become interdependent you must first learn to be independent. Remember you have read about how you should view yourself as a 'whole' person and not rely on others to make you happy.

By being happy with yourself and having confidence and self-esteem you are an independent person. Only once you have learned to be independent can you make the choice to be interdependent.

People who remain dependent on others for their happiness and well-being are individuals who have not learned to be independent.

The power to change is within you and if you use the ABC core techniques you can have and maintain a positive attitude.

I am often asked by individuals how will they know when they have achieved personal development as if it is like a 'course' which has a beginning and an end. The answer is never. Personal development is an on-going process. I continue to learn, to make mistakes, learn from them (or not until a third or fourth time!) but try to regularly use the ABC core techniques. I am not super human and sometimes forget to practice them but soon something negative happens and I have to remind myself that by using the positive techniques I can draw positive things and people to me. They do work.

**8.4 How to become interdependent**

The key to becoming interdependent is self-awareness. You can go back and read the chapter on this again. You should also look at your past conditioning and might want to return to that section. Everyone has had 'programming' of some kind as they grow up, from parents, teachers, authority figures and more. Remember the section on 'labels' and that even positive labels can impact on you in less than favourable way. Read these sections again and while you are thinking that there is so much to take in, just remind yourself that the overall feel good factor can be achieved by regularly using the ABC core techniques and by encouraging yourself which leads nicely to the next chapter.

# CHAPTER 9

# Attribute 5 – Encouragement (and praise)

*Start and end your day with encouragement. Be around and associate with positive people* Patricia Elliot

Some information was given about encouragement and the difference between it and praise in chapter 5. You might want to go back and remind yourself.

The main point is to try to use phrases that build self-image and self-esteem rather than phrases of praise that judge whether you or the individual you are praising is worthy of these words of praise.

Encouragement builds self-esteem. It differs from praise in that it uses descriptive words and this increases internal motivation.

In this chapter I am more concerned with you encouraging yourself and not waiting for someone else to do it for you.

So when encouraging yourself use words that make you feel good about yourself. This allows you to receive your own words of encouragement without judging yourself and what you have done. Even if you do not do a perfect job you can still encourage yourself that you will think about how you would do it next time or you will ask someone to show you. Learning to 'ask how' is detailed in chapter 11 under 'know how'.

If you learn what phrases to use for encouragement and praise then you can use them anywhere. They do make a difference. Just imagine the difference at work or home or among friends.

## 9.1 How to start encouraging yourself

One of the most difficult things to do is to encourage yourself. This is usually because of past conditioning. Go back and remind yourself of how you have been conditioned. You may have been brought up to think it selfish to think of yourself first or think of yourself at all. However if you don't think of and about yourself, who will? So you will need to get rid of past conditioning and start thinking of yourself as being the most important person in your life. If you take care of yourself and think about yourself then you will have more to give yourself and others around you.

It also helps if you associate with positive people. Think for a moment of times when people have put you down and you were upset. Once again no-one should put you down but there will always be those who want to because of their own insecurity and jealousy. Sometimes people don't even like others to be happy. So start by not allowing people to impact on your life in a negative way. You can only get upset if you let people upset you. Affirm that you are important, that you feel good and life is good.

## 9.2 Don't wait for someone else to praise you

Once you learn to encourage and praise yourself you can spread the 'feel good' factor to others. Although I have talked much about 'you' being the most important person in your life, you do not live in isolation. So you need to know the importance of coming together with other positive people and building relationships that are positive.

Many people face challenges in life, in the workplace and even at home. You may be someone who always appears happy and up-beat but the reality is that your home life is not what it should be. No-one really knows what goes on behind closed doors. You can choose to change this by not letting negativity from others impact on you. I know it is easy for me to say that you have choices but you do have even though your choices may be very difficult ones to make.

I can share some personal experience of a difficult choice. I was in a relationship with an extremely possessive man whose behaviour was abusive. The choice was to stay within what appeared to the outside world as 'materially' wealthy surroundings or move for emotional security for my four children and myself. The story is too long to recount here but suffice to say that for years the atmosphere was tense causing all of us to be nervous and suffer psychological damage.

I decided to leave. Naively I thought that the 'material' wealth would be fairly divided as I had worked for years to build our business while bringing up four children. This was not to happen. Again too long a story for this book. However the fact that all of us were immediately more relaxed and happy confirmed that my decision to leave was the right. Of course this did not mean we had no struggles. With little money and a very prolonged court case we faced many challenges. Again this is too long a story for here. If you want to learn more you will need to read my personal book!

So no matter whether home or work in life you do have choices. Some choices will be difficult as you may or will have commitments, mortgage, bills to pay, family and so on, and you need money to pay these bills and also just to live.

When the choice is difficult you can make your life better if you encourage yourself and do the ABC core techniques regularly.

When you feel good about yourself you can take 'a little piece of this feel good factor' into the workplace and to those around you.

It is also good to have cornerstone individuals in your life. Build a 'team' of positive people around you. Try to remove negative people from your life. Again this is difficult if you live with negative people but you can start by telling them that their negative words and behavior are not acceptable to you. If you say this often enough then they will get the message and even want some of what you have – a positive outlook. They may want to learn the ABC core techniques and do these too – the ripple effect!

You will meet many people through life and there are too many types to consider them all in this book. It would be an odd world if we were all the same. However try to associate yourself with the positive ones. The 'law of attraction' kicks in because if you are positive then you will draw such like-minded people to you more and more.

## Some types of individuals

For some fun I list some types of individuals – you may know one or two individuals like this; you may even be one of them! Hopefully you will recognise which ones you should be and which ones you should have around you.

The 'whiz kid' tends to live in the fast lane. They might be charismatic but also arrogant. Then there is the person who is always looking for the next challenge, flitting from one thing to another – I call them the butterfly. Then you might know a solid, dependable character, a 'wise' person you can depend on for solid advice. I call them the 'gold bar'.

Now I am sure you know some individuals of the next type, that is the person who picks your ideas and makes them their own. They are like piranhas. You want to avoid them or if you are one, make a decision now to change.

What about people who have no minds of their own but are two faced. These people are dangerous and you should avoid them. They are the chameleons. Some individuals, particularly in the workplace, are those that suck up to the boss, usually they lack imagination and try to be the 'favourite'.

The status seeker is another in the work place that would do anything for promotion. What about the 'know it all'? This is the person who comes across as if they know it all but are usually pretending to make themselves sound good.

Then there is the 'odd one out'. This is the awkward person who can be shy or they can just be someone who tries to be awkward, asking difficult questions just to upset everyone. At the other end of the spectrum there is the 'mentor' who helps you develop your ability and talent. They are a valuable member of any team.

Do you recognise anyone you know? Probably you will know someone from each of these types and even yourself!

By reading these different types and knowing that you can give yourself permission at all times to encourage yourself and be positive brings me to the next chapter which is about valuing yourself as a person.

Before reading on you might want to go back and look at 'who you are' and your strengths and weaknesses. Do you think you are focusing more on your strengths now that you are using the ABC core techniques? You should be.

*Be selective about your external influences. Your multi-dimensional brain is influenced by everything you see, hear, read, smell, touch, feel or say.* Brian Tracy

CHAPTER 10

# Attribute 6 – Value (and respect)

*The willingness to accept responsibility for one's own life is the source from which self-respect springs.* Joan Didion

In this chapter I address what it means to 'value' yourself. It is not about money as such but to know how to value yourself and others. I call it your driving force towards feeling good. It is about 'respect'

The most important person to value and respect is yourself. If you have read all the previous chapters you should not be finding it difficult to think of yourself first and therefore it should not be difficult for you to think about how much you value yourself.

Value is linked to self-confidence and self-esteem. You have read about these in previous chapters and might want to go back and remind yourself of these topics.

Respect is about feeling worthy and valued. It means taking account of your feelings, needs, thoughts, ideas and therefore when you value and respect others you are taking into consideration their feelings, needs, thoughts, ideas and wishes. This does not mean you are agreeing with everything someone else says or thinks. It just means acknowledging them, listening to them, being truthful with them and accepting them as individuals. You may want to remind yourself of the effective listening model.

Just as I am asking you to consider others, so must you consider yourself. Listen to yourself, your thoughts and ideas. Also remember that everything starts as a thought. As well as feeling valued and respected you can feel value and respect for yourself and from others.

Respect can be shown through behavior. You can act in ways which are respectful. For value and respect to be effective your behaviour should reflect your feelings. When your feeling of value and respect is there your behaviour will naturally reflect this.

Respect has a value which money can't buy. You can sense whether you are respected or not and this is true whether you have money and power or not. Sometimes it is those who pursue money and power who are actually seeking respect.

When you are respected you usually get the voluntary co-operation from other people and normally there are fewer conflicts or matters are resolved more amicably. You also feel better and that makes life better for you and everyone around you.

### 10.1 LEARN HOW TO VALUE AND RESPECT YOURSELF

Learning to value and respect yourself is important because when you do this you find that you get it back. It is a bit like the 'law of attraction' - what you send out comes back to you.

You can learn to value and respect yourself by using the affirmations, the A of the ABC core techniques. Start by saying I value and respect myself.

**Exercise:** write down the affirmation 'I value and respect myself' and then say it three times.

133

Being able to do this can be difficult and this is because of past conditioning. So you may want to return to that section to remind yourself of labels and conditioning. Have you managed to rid yourself of negative labels and challenged your past conditioning? You may have been told or learned that it is selfish to think about yourself. However if you do not take care of yourself then you are not really going to be much use to others! So start looking after yourself. You can tell yourself that you are worthy.

Although respect is something earned you can learn to respect yourself by using the affirmations. You will then find it more natural to respect others. You earn the respect of someone else by voluntarily taking into consideration their feelings, thoughts, ideas, wishes and needs. Once you send it out it will come back to you.

You may have met some people who think they can demand or force you to value and respect them but value and respect are not something you can demand or force.

You can even teach a child what respect is by attending to their natural needs when just a baby. As the baby grows their needs change and they start to express their own views and own preferences. The child increasingly has a need for freedom and independence. If you treat the growing child with increasing respect you will get respect in return. Remind yourself of the section on dependence, independence and inter-dependence.

As children grow up their needs change but you can teach respect and earn respect if the lines of communication are effective and open. You can do this by asking how they feel, empathising with them, trying to understand their feeling and taking their feelings into account. This process is effective if the growing child can express their feelings, know their feelings have value and that feelings matters.

This is a huge topic and I have only touched on it here. I also want to provide some information on the confusion between respect and fear or obedience.

Sometimes parents and teachers believe that if a child obeys them then it means the child respects them. This is a mistaken belief. If you think this then you are mistakenly labeling 'respect' for 'fear' or 'obedience'.

If you have not felt respected by your parents or carers when you were young and living with them then you will have a need to feel respected later in life. This seems obvious but many people have grown up without feeling respected and valued.

If your emotional needs have not been met as a child and you have not felt respected by your parents or carers then you will take things more personally later on in life. You may recognise this in yourself.

Are you someone who makes a huge scene over something which other people see as very small and insignificant? Are you someone who demands respect from your children, sales assistants in the supermarket? Or do you seek a position of power so you have authority over others as a way of trying to get respect. If so, you are confusing respect and fear.

However another consequence of not being respected by your parents or carers is that you will have low self-esteem and low confidence. This is because you do not feel worthy of respect. You will let people take advantage of you, manipulate and abuse you. Manipulation and abuse can be emotional, mental or physical or all three.

Don't worry if you recognise any of this you can change and start to do so by using the ABC core techniques regularly.

It also helps to understand the difference between fear and respect.

Fear is learned. It is like poison. It is toxic. It destroys self-confidence

Respect is earned. It is nurturing and builds self-confidence. Respect enhances your life. However there are and always will be difficult people around that you might need to deal with!

**10.2 How to deal with difficult people**

*Everything that irritates about others can lead us to an understanding about ourselves* Carl Jung

So how do we deal with difficult people? The answer is easy. Avoid them. But I hear you say that's not easy to do – you can't just leave work, walk out of your home and family and so on. So dealing with difficult people really depends on who these difficult people are and how often you have to interact with them.

If it is someone you are not likely to meet again or interact with often then you can avoid them in the future but while with them you can switch off your emotions and not get into a deep conversation with them, then keep the meeting short by excusing yourself politely. Then walk away.

However if it is someone you interact with often such as co-worker, partner, friend and so on you need to learn ways of dealing with difficult people.

If you work with, live with, deal with difficult people you will know that it is time consuming and emotionally draining.

First of all if you are working with or living with people who upset you or make you angry you need to remember that you can only get upset or angry if you let them upset you or make you angry. So this is about taking control of your life. If you spend your life being upset, angry or hurt because of the behaviour of others then you have given up control over your life.

Now I know that there is no perfect world out there and almost everyone will have had to deal with difficult people at some time in life. If you are dealing with a difficult person at work then you have to take control and tell them that their behaviour, words or actions are not acceptable. A good way of dealing with heated or angry situations is to leave any discussion until everyone is more calm or till the end of the day, or even the next day when everyone has had time to think and calm down.

Remind yourself of the effective listening model whereby you can acknowledge with noises such as 'mmh', even indicating empathy but do little. If you feel you need to do more then you can acknowledge what the person is good at and leave the rest for another time or altogether.

There are many difficult people out there. You may be one of them. Look back at 'who you are' and your weaknesses. Are you working to diminish these and focus on your strengths?

*Life's challenges are not supposed to paralyse*
*you, they are supposed to help you discover*
*who you are* Bernice Johnson Reagon

Sometimes the difficult person does not even realise that their behaviour is unacceptable so they need to be told. This takes courage. This may be the one brave thing you need to do today. Remind yourself of courage under the chapter on 'audacity'. Hopefully you are now recognising that the attributes are all inter-linked.

You will be good at dealing with difficult people if you are a good listener and effective communicator. You ask open questions allowing space for the difficult person to talk. You also treat a difficult person in the same way as you treat everyone else and you do not avoid them. You will try to see the difficult person's point of view. If you use the effective listening model then you know that by using the four steps you are not accepting what the difficult person is saying but acknowledging their point of view and taking their feelings, thoughts and ideas into consideration. As far as the difficult person is concerned their issues are very real to them.

If you are brave enough and manage to tell the difficult person that their behaviour is not acceptable you must make sure that this is not taken by them to mean that they are a bad person. You also must not take this as a personal issue because it is often the case that difficult people are difficult with everyone.

The behaviour of difficult people is often linked to fear. They behave in this way out of some kind of fear. You will not know what they are afraid of and sometimes even they will not know. If you try to get to the root of the matter you are more likely to find resolution.

If you are someone who is good at dealing with difficult people you may do so because you are able to find clues as to what is annoying them and therefore are able to resolve the problem in a reasonable manner. You will try to build trust and confidence with and in the difficult person.

Sometimes the answer is very simple – just ask them what it is they are looking for so that you can try to find a solution. Probably no-one has ever asked them before. Often a difficult person just wants to feel part of the team, to feel worthy and valued. You can encourage them just like you did for yourself. Everyone wants to feel valued and respected. Research shows that employees rate being valued at work more than money.

Difficult people exist everywhere and I think every workplace has them. However what is important is not the difficult person but how you deal with them that matters. This will depend on your self-esteem and self-confidence. You can go back and remind yourself about these topics.

If you are working with or living with a difficult person then you must deal with that person because your situation will not get better by ignoring it or leaving it unaddressed. In fact usually matters get worse. The most effective way of addressing a difficult person is to be and maintain objectivity and emotional control.

Remember that you cannot change others but you can change yourself. You are doing this by using the ABC core techniques to make a difference to your life so can they!

The difficult person can even turn into a champion for others. Try sharing a laugh – remember laughter is the best medicine.

Difficult people are another of life's challenges and as you are learning from this book challenges should be seen as opportunities.

*In the middle of every difficulty lies opportunity* Albert Einstein

Of course if you don't know, then ask and that leads you to the next chapter 'know how'.

CHAPTER 11

# Attribute 7 – Know How

*You can only understand others if you first
understand yourself* Patricia Elliot

## 11.1 WHAT IS THE 'KNOW HOW' ATTRIBUTE?

What I mean by 'know how' is being able to ask questions and find out more information no matter the topic. Never be afraid to learn and discover more about yourself, others and the world around you.

Look back at 'who you are' and look again at your strengths and weaknesses. Now ask yourself some questions. Do you recognise your strengths, do you know your weaknesses and are you trying to decrease and even lose them?

Do you recognise your work colleagues, your friends, your family and do you know their strengths and weaknesses?

Do you find yourself being able to tell others that their behaviour is not acceptable to you?

If you are using and continue to use the ABC core techniques you should be feeling, acting and living in a much more positive way. You may have met with opposition from others, even those close to you but as long as you know that this is their problem not yours you can continue to move towards improving your overall well-being.

People do not like change. They fear change and as you are becoming different this is a change and therefore they are frightened of this. Hopefully if these are people close to you then you can open up and share the techniques. But remember you cannot change them. Only they can change themselves but they have to be open to the idea.

## 11.2 NEVER BE AFRAID TO FIND OUT OR ASK

*It's not what you know, it's what you use*
*that makes a difference.* Zig Ziglar

Sometimes it takes a lot of courage and confidence to speak out and ask a question if you are unsure or don't know the answer. You have to be brave. Have you ever listened to someone and not known what they were talking about? This often happens when people use jargon when they talk. I remember when I started a new job I had to attend an induction and jargon was used to explain what each department did and so on. Eventually I plucked up courage to ask what some of the jargon meant and I was astounded to find that the speaker could not explain their own jargon.

Now my intention in asking the question was not to embarrass the speaker but to try to find out what she was talking about. Later when I asked the others at the meeting whether they knew the jargon they all said that they were glad I had asked the question as they didn't know what she was talking about either!

Never set out to embarrass anyone. You never know when the tables might be turned!

My first fairly terrifying job as a young lawyer was when I had to give a lecture to some construction site workers. Most of them were considerably older than me and certainly knew their environment. I had never worked on a construction site. So I knew that it would be challenging and it was. I decided that I had to get the audience on my side. This tip has stood me in good stead over the years. I did this by asking them for their experiences and they were only too pleased to oblige.

Most of my first lecture was taken up with them doing the talking. The feedback I got was great. They said I had been really excellent (and yet they had done most of the talking!). Just shows you that when you do the listening, the talker thinks that they have had a great conversation!

Of course I realised that I could not let them talk through every lecture. I also knew that they were eager to challenge me and my knowledge. Now I have some specialist subjects but even so, one individual cannot know everything about everything!!

So what do you do when, as a supposed expert, you are faced with a question which you can't answer?

I asked some students a short time ago and a few said, blag it, just ignore the question and so on. Well that is what not to do!

Honesty is the best policy. So when asked something I did not know the answer to, that is exactly what I said. I don't know. However I did add that I would know where to find the answer. In fact I turned the situation around into a learning experience for the students. I would say to the students. That's an excellent question. I don't know the answer as I can't know everything about the law but let's see if we can all try to find the answer and discuss it at the next lecture.

This has proved to be an invaluable method of dealing with difficulties. In almost every walk of life there will always be some 'smart alec' who wants to challenge you and your knowledge. So try my method next time you are challenged. It also takes the 'steam' out of a situation which could be confrontational.

Of course never confuse not knowing everything from not preparing. You should always prepare to the best of your ability and with all the tools and resources you have available to you.

A quick reality check is to be prepared, be aware, be objective and have as much information as possible to face the situation at hand.

In addition to my daily routine of the ABC core techniques I use them before facing an audience and any challenges.

*I aim through this book and the ABC core techniques to help you recognise your potential so you can help yourself to be the best you can be no matter the situation.* Patricia Elliot

CHAPTER 12

# Summary and overview

In this chapter I summarise and provide an overview of the ABC core techniques again and why systematic repetition is vital to their effective use and your success; and then provide a brief summary again of each of the 7 Attributes

Awareness (self-awareness)
Resilience
Audacity
De-attachment
Encouragement
Value motive/respect
Know how

Hopefully you are using my ABC core techniques regularly and know that they are easy to learn and easy to use. You may be using one technique more than another or finding that all three together work well. No matter whether you are using the Affirmations, Breathing and Creative Imagery together or separately they are proven psychological techniques and if repeated regularly and at particularly challenging times, they do work.

Very briefly 'A' stands for affirmation which is about positive thinking, attitudes and behaviour; turning negatives into positives; seeing challenges as opportunities.

'B' is for breathing but not just your everyday breathing but effective breathing which help reduce and manage stress and help you deal with life's challenges by providing you with more energy to do so.

The third core technique but by no means the last is 'C' for creative imagery or also known as visualisations. You may have been used to doing this but if not hopefully you are finding it easy to do so now. You might want to take time to recognise which 'sense' you use most or do you use all five of your senses?

For the ABC core techniques to be successful and effective you should be practicing them and repeated them. This is called systematic repetition. If you have been following this method then the ABC core techniques will have become part of your daily routine. They will now be part of your good habits. You should be feeling and continue to feel the benefits of reduced stress and overall improved well-being.

You will recall there was some information in chapter 4 on stress. Hopefully by using and repeating the core techniques, the only stress you should be experiencing is the constructive kind!

Chapter 5 then moved on to detail the first attribute, awareness. You may want to look again at the shapes to see if you are focusing more on your strengths. Were you able to challenge your past conditioning and get rid of some of those labels?

You will realise of course that it is not easy to stay positive and this is where the next attribute comes in. You have to be resilient, able to bounce back against adversity. This was discussed in chapter 6. Hopefully you now know that you can face challenges and push against the barriers of adversity. If you meet that 'wall' you will want to find a way round, or over, or right through. This type of action takes courage and you learned about this in chapter 7.

Audacity is the third attribute and is about being brave and courageous. Not necessarily doing something huge but even small things which help you towards a new positive you. However despite having and learning about these attributes you also needed to know when to 'let go' and not be so attached to something or someone that it impedes you in your progress through life. So you learned about what it is to de-attach in chapter 8.

De-attachment, the fourth attribute may have been the most difficult to understand but hopefully you have understood that it is one of the most helpful in dealing with relationships and people. It is not about being aloof or apart from others and it is not about being so dependent that you cannot be without the other person or other 'thing'. You read about jealousy and possessiveness which cause many relationships to break down and learned how to become more inter-dependent. However to do this you probably needed encouragement and you learned how to do this for yourself in chapter 9.

The fifth attribute, encouragement, was discussed in chapter 9 and you will know now that you start with yourself. You encourage yourself and do not to wait for someone else to praise you but by doing this you learn more easily to praise others. By doing this the world around you becomes a better place to live in.

In addition to encouraging yourself you learned about how to value and respect yourself. This was discussed in chapter 10. By reading about this you hopefully will recognise your feelings and that you may not have had respect when growing up. However you know that you can learn to respect yourself and how to respect others. You also learned some ways of dealing with difficult people.

The final attribute, 'know how', was discussed in chapter 11. You learned that if you 'don't know' you can use the 'know how' to find out.

Now there are many ways of reading this book. You may have reached this point by reading each chapter in sequence or having read some self-help type books you may have decided to read a chapter that most interests you. No matter what, I hope you have read and continue to do so with an open heart and mind. Remember too that when I talk of success I mean inner success, emotional success, not the material kind but you can never tell what comes from thinking and behaving positively.

I do hope that unlike other books you are not going to put this on a shelf to gather dust. I want it to be like a 'friend on the shoulder' to lift and lay when you need or want to help you along the way to a truly successful way of life, mentally and emotionally.

I also hope that by reading the book and using my ABC core techniques you are finding out who you are, how to change your thoughts from negative to positive, how to shift or change your 'paradigm (pattern)', challenge your beliefs, identify your choices and clarify your vision.

When used, my ABC core techniques do work especially in stressful times. Just take a few small steps every day.

*A journey of a thousand miles, starts with one small step.* Chinese proverb

# APPENDIX I

## Exercises and Examples

**AFFIRMATIONS – some examples**

**Love**
I love myself
I act lovingly towards others

**Self confidence and growth**
I am self confident
I am responsible for myself
I am the best I can be

**Self trust**
I trust myself
I do my best at all times
I treat each day as a new day

**Taking action**
I accept changes
I am successful
I am creative

**Inner strength and courage**
I have courage
I handle things positively
I take responsibility for my life

**Awareness**
I am self-aware
I am open to those around me

**Intuition**
I use my intuition
I see the positive side of situations

**My inner wisdom**
I have inner wisdom
I see challenges as opportunities for growth

**Wonders of life**
I see the wonders of nature all around

**Creating happiness**
I make a positive difference to those around me
I turn challenges into positive opportunities for myself and others around me
**Relationships with self and others**
I have a happy relationships with myself
I attract positive people to me
**Sharing and giving**
I attract good things in life to me
I smile and am happy with life

## AFFIRMATIONS - Exercises

### 3-2-1 Exercise
If you are new to saying or making up affirmations then this 3 step exercise will help.

**Instructions**

Step 1: say the affirmation in the 3rd person (3). By doing this it feels as if you are talking about someone else.

Step 2: after saying the affirmation in the 3rd person two or three times, you can then move on to saying it in the 2nd person (2). This still removes the affirmation from being too personal to YOU.

Step 3: the final step is to say the affirmation in the 1st person(1). By doing the first 2 steps once or twice you can move on to say it in the 1st person as you should be more comfortable with it being truly YOU. Then practice, say and repeat. You will discover it really works.

Remember your affirmations are further small steps in your new journey. The most effective method is to repeat them until they become a habit.

Before going on to do the 3-2-1 exercise read the next paragraph and then do the 'optional writing' exercise.

Write out the affirmation 2 or 3 times together with a response (your response is whatever thought or feeling is present at that point – it may even be a negative response. Do not worry).

Once your affirmation becomes a habit, it will be second nature to you and this 'writing' exercise will be optional. You will eventually just use the '1st person' and your response and feeling will be positive.

Research shows that it does not matter if you believe your affirmation it still helps you to be positive. Just say it with feeling. It is obviously wonderful if you do believe it!

Now try the 'optional writing' exercise below.

**Exercise: The Optional Writing**

Use the affirmation – 'I feel good'

Now respond to this. Your response can be anything for example:

- this is nonsense.....or
- I wish this were true.........or

- I enjoy writing this...... or
- this is true........etc.

Once you have done this you can try the 3-2-1 exercise below.

**Exercise: 3-2-1 affirmation exercise**.

Remember the purpose of this is to introduce you gently to being able to say your own personal affirmations using the 3Ps principle you read about in chapter 2. Now try the exercise below.

Step 1: you are going to write down your affirmation in the $3^{rd}$ person 3 times. So if your name is Alan, then you would write down the affirmation as follows:-

Alan feels good. So using your own name, write down your affirmation 3 times on the lines below.

Now respond to this statement, for example, 'Alan thinks this is silly' or better still, try responding positively, for example, 'Alan does feel good'.

Step 2: you are going to write down your affirmation in the $2^{nd}$ person 3 times. So again using your own name, for example if you name is Alan, then you would write down the affirmation as follows:-

'Alan, you feel good' OR you could just write 'You feel good'. Now write down the affirmation 3 times on the lines below.

Now respond to this statement, for example, 'You think this is silly don't you' or better still, try responding positively, for example, 'you feel better don't' you'.

Step 3: you are now going to write the affirmation down 3 times in the first person, for example, no matter your name, you will write down 3 times 'I feel good' on the lines below.

Now respond to this statement, for example, 'I feel silly' or better still, try responding positively, for example, 'I feel good'.

## BREATHING - Exercises

### Q-BREATHING EXERCISE

Read the exercise below until you are ready to do it. Then try it with your eyes open and then once familiar with it, close your eyes and do it again. The new Qvolution program will have video clips but meanwhile the exercise is explained below.

| Body part | Approx Time | Procedure for the exercise |
|---|---|---|
| | | |
| Toes | 5 secs | Feel and focus on your toes by holding them tightly, then release and relax them, wiggling your toes |
| | | |
| Ankles | 5 secs | Pull your toes towards your head, focus on your ankles, hold for 5 seconds and then relax |
| | | |
| Legs | 9 secs | Stretch your legs stiffly, focus on them, firstly at the calf for 3 seconds then relax, then the knees for 3 seconds then relax, then the thighs for 3 seconds then relax |
| | | |
| Arms | 10 secs | Stretch your arms straight in front, pull hands and fingers together. Hold for 10 seconds and then relax |
| | | |
| Shoulders | 12 secs | Pull your shoulders up towards your ears. Hold for 4 seconds and then relax slowly, breathing out as you relax. Repeat twice. |

| | | |
|---|---|---|
| **Face** | 12 secs | Balance your head squarely on your shoulders to release any tension in the neck area. Screw your face up tightly. Hold for 12 seconds, then relax. Unclench your teeth and open your mouth slightly, relaxing it. Repeat twice |
| | | |
| **Eyes** | 5 secs | Lightly close your eyes, then tightly shut them, then relax the eyelids. This is the finishing part of the exercise. |

I, and many of my clients, find this exercise very helpful in times of stress and anxiety. I also recommend that you do it even when not stressed.

Do not do this exercise while driving or operating machinery.

**Exercise – find out if you are breathing for best health**

Breathing in through your nose, breathe smoothly. Take notice of your natural breath pattern. Ask yourself if your breath is going into your abdominal cavity or upper chest, or sides of your rib cage or the back of your rib cage.

If you find that your breath is going into your upper chest, you may be lifting your shoulders as you breathe, then you should lie down and try the exercise again. Take notice of your natural breath pattern. If your breath is still going into the upper chest then you are still not breathing as effectively as you should be. Now try the next exercise.

**Exercise – Efficient breathing exercise**

Have a scarf ready. Lie on your back on the floor. Relax your neck and shoulders, feel as if they are blending into the floor.

Bend your knees up so that your feet are flat on the floor. Your knees should be together and can keep them together by tying a scarf round your thighs just near the knees.

Place your hands at the side of your rib cage. You do this so that you can feel what is happening when you breathe in and out. You are now going to imagine that your ribcage is a balloon. When you inhale this balloon will inflate. Now start to breathe in through your nose. Feel your hands move outward – this is the balloon inflating.

Now exhale, letting your breath out slowly and the balloon should deflate – you should feel your hands moving inwards and your stomach (front) of your body should go inward towards your back. As you are lying on your back your neck and shoulders should be relaxed.

This is efficient breathing. Now you can try this exercise while standing up. Place your hands on the sides of your ribcage with your fingers towards the back of your ribcage. Let your hands feel your ribcage go out and in (out when you inhale and in when you exhale). You should use some muscular effort to pull in your lower tummy muscles. For those who do Pilates, this is known as 'scooping' or 'navel to spine'.

Practice again and again. Another place to practice is when lying in bed just before going to sleep.

**Breathing fundamentals**

Just because one particular breathing exercise or development technique feels good does not mean it is the best choice. Many feel good at the outset of a certain exercise but that is largely because so many breathe so poorly that any progress feels significant, and it may well be. But each technique or exercise must be based in solid breathing fundamentals otherwise they can work against each other and cause future breathing development problems. Like a rocket ship even slightly off course, as the days and weeks pass, you will travel further and further away from your goal of a long, healthy, vibrant life. Knowing the fundamentals helps you stay on course.

### Chest Breathing

Chest breathing, or more specifically, high chest dominant breathing, often causes and can worsen chest pain.

**Mirror Exercise:** Stand and look into a mirror or close your eyes and feel what occurs or ask someone to observe you.

Put your right hand on your belly and your left hand on your chest. Take a very deep breath, as deep as you can. When you breathe in very deeply:

Do you raise your rib cage?

Do you raise your shoulders?

Do your neck muscles bulge out?

Then you used your chest too much to breathe.

Try it again with a quick breath (sniff) through your nose. Did the hand on your belly move? If not then you used your chest too much to breathe.

When you get challenged or stressed your breathing pattern can and usually does head upwards to the chest.

### Timing Exercise

Take a watch with a second hand and breathe for 60 seconds (1 minute), counting from 1 upwards for each 'in/out' breathe. After 60 seconds, stop and ask yourself how many breaths did you take?

Was it
- 30 or over?
- between 20 and 30?
- between 10 and 20?
- Or under 10?

If you were under 10 then you are probably doing efficient breathing. Those who take part in yoga, or athletics, or are trained in singing, drama or speaking are usually taught how to breathe efficiently.

## CREATIVE IMAGERY OR VISUALISATION TITLES

**Explanation of creative imagery/visualisation**

Over the years many people have told me that they find it difficult to visualise. I decided to find out why by speaking to many individuals. I discovered it was because of the use of certain words such as 'see' the clouds or 'see' the sea or grass and so on. The difficulty arises because individuals are unique and visualise or imagine in different ways.

There are five senses and some people use one sense, others another. So I decided to change the way creative imagery was used, spoken or read.

So to use creative imagery or visualise means to imagine using one or all of the five senses e.g.

- Some people imagine through touch
- Some through smell
- Some through hearing
- Some through seeing
- Some through taste

To find out what sense or senses you use to visualise try this simple exercise.

**Exercise**

Imagine a recent happy event. Relax and breathe deeply. Think of this event for a moment or two. Close your eyes. Say for example this event is a holiday by the sea. Do you:-

- 'hear' the sea (the waves crashing or water lapping
- 'see' the colour of the waves (blue, green, grey, white surf)
- 'feel' the water (cool, warm, crashing against your legs or lapping against your legs)
- 'smell' the freshness of the sea air (salty, fresh, fishy)
- 'taste' the water (salty sea, salty air on your lips)

How do you respond to it? Is it by:-

- hearing the silence
- seeing the beauty
- feeling as if you could touch the water
- smelling the ferns and the wild flowers
- tasting the purity of the air

Remember you may use more than one sense and might even use all your senses. Creative imagery or visualisation is best if you are able to close your eyes while doing the exercise. Some visualisations are provided below and there will be imagery and music in the new version of Qvolution.

The visualisations are short enough for you to read, remember and then close your eyes and actually do them. Creative imagery is the 'C' of the ABC core techniques. Creative imagery or visualisation is a powerful strategy for everyday living. You will become expert and can make up your own. Now try to imagine something positive or choose one from the list of visualisations below. I intend to add to these in the new Qvolution program and also welcome your suggestions.

## THE GOLDEN SPHERE

Imagine yourself standing on sun drenched sand. Feel the sun on your face. Feel the warmth. You feel relaxed. On your right there is a large golden sphere. Step inside. Feel the warmth all around you. Feel warm and relaxed. A feeling of calm engulfs you. You know that you are safe. Hold this feeling within you.

## A SAFE PLACE

Imagine yourself in a place that you like to be. It can be anywhere. It is somewhere you like to go to dream or just sit. Imagine your surroundings. You feel safe. No-one can enter this safe place unless you want them to. You are comfortable just being there. You have no fears when you are there. This is your safe place. Hold this picture in your mind.

OR this next one which is very good for calming you. However if you are afraid of water then just choose another one.

## CALM LAKE

Imagine you are on a small boat. The sun is shining down. You feel so relaxed. The water is like a mirror. Flat and calm. Lie back. Close your eyes. Feel the heat of the sun. Listen. There is no sound. Enjoy the rest and tranquility. Your mind is now at peace. Hold this peace within you.

## THE BEACH

Imagine you are walking on golden sand – stretching far into the distance. You feel free. Space is all around you. Stretching far into the distance is the horizon. There is only this peaceful scene. Sand, sea and open space. You move forward with a sense of freedom and self confidence.

## THE MEADOW AND THE TREE

Imagine yourself out in the countryside. You are walking across this lovely meadow. The air around you is so pure. In the centre of the meadow there is a large solid tree. It has luscious green branches draping down. Rest at this strong tree. Lean against the bark. Feel the security. The energy. You feel safe. Rest for another moment. You feel strong and confident.

## FLOATING CLOUDS

Imagine yourself sitting quietly. Breathe deeply. Imagine soft white clouds. Slowly floating by. Focus on how delicate and fine they are. You feel a sense of lightness. Your mind is calm.

Your body is calm. You have more awareness. Slowly open your eyes and bring yourself back into where you are now. You feel calm and peaceful.

## GOLDEN SUNSET

Imagine yourself watching the setting of the golden sun. Still vibrant and vivid as the rays slowly fade below the horizon. Feel contentment rise within you knowing that a new day will dawn tomorrow. You feel warm and content.

## GARDEN FLOWERS

Imagine yourself in a lovely garden. Take a minute or two to admire the flowers. Their beauty. The glorious colours. The wonderful scent. Think about your own favourite flower. Think of the changing seasons. Pause and think again of the glorious array and how it changes with the seasons. You feel confident and know that you can face any change.

## THE HORIZON

Take time to reflect. Imagine yourself to be somewhere you enjoy. A place of natural beauty. Imagine the sand and sea grasses the view extending to the horizon beyond. Ever changing just like life. Take a minute to use all your senses – feel the sand in your toes, touch the grass, smell the sea air, listen to the waves, imagine the beauty all around you. Quietly reflect. Look again to the horizon. Continue your journey with confidence.

## COLOURS OF THE RAINBOW

Imagine yourself watching the fiery red of the setting sun, vibrant and vivid, slowly watch as it fades to orange, and then yellow as it disappear from view, now imagine yourself on a carpet of green grass, feel the dew of dawn, as you waken to a clear blue sky, you lie content watching the clouds float by, falling asleep you waken to the sky deepening to indigo/violet contrasting with the silvery pale of the moon, you are calm and peaceful, relax for a moment, breathe deeply. You feel relaxed and calm. You know you can influence yourself and others positively.

I provide below some detail on the colours.

## BACKGROUND OF THE RAINBOW COLOURS

Although colours can be associated with some negative emotions, such as 'red' which is often associated with 'anger'. I do not use the colours in any negative way. I focus instead on the positive aspects of the colours which can help with or overcome certain emotions and feelings.

Red: helps overcome negative thoughts

Orange: helps raise your self-esteem and free your emotions, stimulates your interest in life

Yellow: helps you to use your intuition, to have clarity of thought, to assimilate new ideas, to build your confidence and to be more optimistic

Green: helps you to de-stress, to be calm and relaxed particularly in relationships with yourself and others

Blue: helps you to communicate effectively, to soothe and calm you and inspire your creativity

Indigo: helps calm your nerves

Violet: helps balance your mind

### Exercise: Rainbow ribbons

I use this exercise to help people let go of problems and challenges, particularly ones over which they have no control.

Sit quietly with your feet firmly on the ground. You must be comfortable and relaxed. Close your eyes. Take a few deep breaths. Now think of a challenge you face just now (it can be anything, life, work, home, big, small – it does not matter). Once you have the challenge in your head, without thinking put a colour to it. Immediately it is surrounded by this colour. Now imagine the colour is a ribbon or a balloon. Your challenge is now this ribbon or balloon. Relax and take a few deep breaths. Now let go of the ribbon or balloon, see it floating away and say to yourself 3 times - 'I let go of this problem, I let go of this problem, I let go of this problem'. As you are saying these words, the ribbon or balloon is floating away and it is gone. You say to yourself 3 times I feel relaxed and positive. I feel relaxed and positive. I feel relaxed and positive. I have let go of this problem.

If you find yourself still worrying, then do the exercise again but this time surround the 'problem' in a bright yellow light and then let it go. Keep doing this. Keep affirming. You will feel better. I have had many people do this and feedback is always positive and that they feel better.

Why hold on to a problem over which you have no control.

If you wish to know more about the colour you have chosen then please feel free to contact me via the websites www.mindcircles.co.uk or www.patriciaelliot.com

## SYSTEMATIC REPETITION (HABITS)

**List of bad and good habits (just in case you can't think of any!)**

I am sure this list jogs your memory and you might even want to add some of your own! I have included both physical and mental/emotional habits too.

| Bad habits (physical) | Good habits (physical) |
|---|---|
| Smoking | Eating healthily |
| Drinking/taking too much caffeine | Taking time for yourself |
| Eating with your mouth open | Taking healthy exercise |

| | |
|---|---|
| Speaking with your mouth full | Tidying up after yourself |
| Watching too much television | Clearing clutter |
| Nail-biting | Having set place for keys (house, car) |
| Cracking your knuckles/ bones | Making your bed |
| Belching | Putting something back after use |
| Bragging | Setting a routine to prevent stress |
| Fidgeting | Paying bills on time |
| Gossiping | Budgeting with money |
| Getting angry | Designating a set place for bills |
| Drug abuse | Not ignoring problems/debt |
| Gambling | Making shopping list and sticking to it |
| Taking sleeping pills | Being assertive |
| Bulimia | |
| Anorexia | |
| Aggressive (physical) | |

| **Mental/emotional bad habits** | **Mental/Emotional good habits** |
|---|---|
| Too busy to listen to others | Being caring |
| Being a know-it-all | Being a good listener |
| Being critical | Being calm under pressure |

| | |
|---|---|
| Being anxious | Preventing stress before it becomes a problem |
| Always complaining | Being considerate of others |
| Worrying | Valuing yourself |
| Arguing | Respecting others |
| Being jealous | Assertive manner |
| Being shy | |
| Being lazy | |
| Continually being late | |
| Aggressive (mental/ emotional) | |

This book aims to help you identify your bad habits and is intended to help you stop bad habits. However, the information provided is not a 'cure' and if you are having difficulties with any habits, particularly the serious ones I recommend that you seek appropriate medical/counseling/professional assistance.

**Habits – good and bad habits exercise**
Step 1: identify your habits by making a list of your good and bad habits. Draw 2 columns, good in one column and bad in the other.

Step 2: the first small step to improve your life is to choose 'one' bad habit which you are going to decide not to practice.

Step 3: re-inforce your decision to change your way of practicing habits by writing down the bad habit that you want to stop practicing.

Step 4: write down how this one bad habit has affected you and those around you. Ask yourself what were and are the consequences of continuing to practice this bad habit?

Step 5: ask yourself why you continue to practice this bad habit. What is holding you back from stopping this bad habit and forming a new habit?

Step 6: take the pressure off yourself by taking only small steps. Don't set yourself unrealistic difficult goals. Don't beat yourself up if you falter at the first step. Encourage yourself. Praise yourself often when you do succeed.

Step 7: you can support yourself further by writing down a positive statement, that is, an affirmation, to support you in your progress. For example it might be 'I eat healthily'.

*Note:* Where necessary seek out support from experts, medical professionals, support individuals or groups.

**(Notes)**

## STRESS SYMPTOMS AND THE DIFFERENT AREAS THAT ARE AFFECTED

| Cognitive Symptoms | Emotional Symptoms |
| --- | --- |
| • Memory problems<br>• Indecisiveness<br>• Inability to concentrate<br>• Trouble thinking clearly<br>• Poor judgment<br>• Seeing only the negative<br>• Anxious or racing thoughts<br>• Constant worrying<br>• Loss of objectivity<br>• Fearful anticipation | • Moodiness<br>• Agitation<br>• Restlessness<br>• Short temper<br>• Irritability, impatience<br>• Inability to relax<br>• Feeling tense and "on edge"<br>• Feeling overwhelmed<br>• Sense of loneliness and isolation<br>• Depression or general unhappiness |

| Physical Symptoms | Behavioral Symptoms |
|---|---|
| • Headaches or backaches<br>• Muscle tension and stiffness<br>• Diarrhea or constipation<br>• Nausea, dizziness<br>• Insomnia<br>• Chest pain, rapid heartbeat<br>• Weight gain or loss<br>• Skin breakouts (hives, eczema)<br>• Loss of sex drive<br>• Frequent colds | • Eating more or less<br>• Sleeping too much or too little<br>• Isolating yourself from others<br>• Procrastination, neglecting responsibilities<br>• Using alcohol, cigarettes, or drugs to relax<br>• Nervous habits (e.g. nail biting, pacing)<br>• Teeth grinding or jaw clenching<br>• Overdoing activities (e.g. exercising, shopping)<br>• Overreacting to unexpected problems<br>• Picking fights with others |

## LIFE EVENTS STRESS SCALE

**Adapted from Holmes-Rahe *Social Readjustment Rating Scale*, Journal of Psychosomatic Research, Vol 11, 1967**
**Life Event** Mean Value

| No. | Event description | Points |
|---|---|---|
| 1 | Death of spouse | 100 |
| 2 | Divorce | 73 |
| 3 | Marital Separation from mate | 65 |
| 4 | Detention in jail or other institution | 63 |

| 5 | Death of a close family member | 63 |
|---|---|---|
| 6 | Major personal injury or illness | 53 |
| 7 | Marriage | 50 |
| 8 | Being fired at work | 47 |
| 9 | Marital reconciliation with mate | 45 |
| 10 | Retirement from work | 45 |
| 11 | Major change in the health or behaviour of a family member | 44 |
| 12 | Pregnancy | 40 |
| 13 | Sexual Difficulties | 39 |
| 14 | Gaining a new family member (i.e. birth, adoption, older adult moving in, etc) | 39 |
| 15 | Major business readjustment | 39 |
| 16 | Major change in financial state (i.e. a lot worse or better off than usual) | 38 |
| 17 | Death of a close friend | 37 |
| 18 | Changing to a different line of work | 36 |
| 19 | Major change in the number of arguments with partner/spouse (i.e. either a lot more or a lot less than usual regarding child rearing, personal habits, etc.) | 35 |
| 20 | Taking on a mortgage (for home, business, etc.) | 31 |
| 21 | Foreclosure on a mortgage or loan | 30 |
| 22 | Major change in responsibilities at work (i.e. promotion, demotion, etc.) | 29 |
| 23 | Son or daughter leaving home (marriage, attending college, joined the forces.) | 29 |
| 24 | In-law troubles | 29 |

| 25 | Outstanding personal achievement | 28 |
| 26 | Spouse beginning or ceasing work outside the home | 26 |
| 27 | Beginning or ceasing formal schooling | 26 |
| 28 | Major change in living condition (new home, refurbishing, deterioration of neighbourhood or home etc.) | 25 |
| 29 | Revision of personal habits (dress manners, associations, quitting smoking) | 24 |
| 30 | Troubles with the boss | 23 |
| 31 | Major changes in working hours or conditions | 20 |
| 32 | Changes in residence | 20 |
| 33 | Changing to a new school | 20 |
| 34 | Major change in usual type and/or amount of recreation | 19 |
| 35 | Major change in church activity (i.e.. a lot more or less than usual) | 19 |
| 36 | Major change in social activities (clubs, movies, visiting, etc.) | 18 |
| 37 | Taking on a loan (car, TV, freezer, etc) | 17 |
| 38 | Major change in sleeping habits (a lot more or a lot less than usual) | 16 |
| 39 | Major change in number of family get-togethers | 15 |
| 40 | Major change in eating habits (a lot more or less food intake, or very different meal hours or surroundings) | 15 |

| 41 | Vacation | 13 |
| 42 | Major holidays | 12 |
| 43 | Minor violations of the law (traffic tickets, jaywalking, disturbing the peace, etc) | 11 |

**300pts or more** raises the odds of being stressed to about 80%, according to the Holmes-Rahe statistical prediction model.

**INSTRUCTIONS: Mark down the point value of each of these life events that has happened to you during the previous year. Total these associated points.**

**Now, add up all the points you have to find your score.**

**150pts or less** means a relatively low amount of life change and a low susceptibility to stress-induced health breakdown.

**150 to 300 pts** implies about a 50% chance of a major health breakdown in the next 2 years.

> *Tip: No matter your points, I would still opt for prevention of stress! I promote doing ABC core techniques to keep you feeling good.*

Sources: Adapted from Thomas Holmes and Richard Rahe. Homes-Rahe Social Readjustment Rating Scale, Journal of Psychosomatic Research. Vol II, 1967.

# Testimonials

I was asked to chair a prestigious event where there would be many people including celebrities. Although I had spoke before a local committee level this was my first time at such an event. I was naturally nervous about being on stage in front of so many people. I decided to use the Qvolution ABC techniques which I had learned such as the breathing and then imagining myself up on stage being confident and positive. I took a few deep breaths and affirmed that I was confident and that event was successful. I added to this positive effect by doing the 'golden sphere' protective visualisation. I knew it would calm me and make me feel secure. I pictured myself standing on the stage inside the golden sphere all around me. I felt calm and confident. The whole evening was a great success and people congratulated me on my natural talent for the stage! Little did they know how I had brought confidence to myself. Jean F.

I was Senior Partner in a large law firm. I had many responsibilities and to relax at the weekends I went sailing. The times I enjoyed the most were when the sea was calm. I used to call it a flat calm. The water was like a mirror and there was no noise. I would just lie back and enjoy the peace. It was this picture that I kept in my mind when I was back in the office surrounded by paperwork and busy atmosphere. If I found myself overwhelmed and getting too stressed or the people around me were uptight I would just picture myself on the calm water with no noise. This brought me immediate peace and calm and I felt relaxed. Robert W. (Solicitor).

As a child when I felt scared or frightened I just pictured myself in my special place. I could go there and dream. I could talk over what had upset or frightened me. Just speaking (out loud or in my head) helped me. I felt safe and I felt I could face anything. As an adult I continue to use this technique. So if anything upsets me or makes me anxious I take myself off 'in my mind' to that special place. I can go there at any time. Even better than that, because I do this in my mind no-one knows I am there! Although it is in my head it is so vivid I feel as if I am there. Pat W. (Self-employed Consultant).

Dealing with full time work as well as returning to study at University brought new challenges. I was worried about juggling family life, work, study and meeting new people who would probably be younger than me. I started picturing myself in a wonderful place, calm and relaxed and it made me feel more positive. At first I thought I would not have time to do this but it is so short yet so effective. I recommend everyone to do this visualisation if they are facing challenges of any kind. I picture myself successfully finishing my University course and having my degree. Mary R. (OU student).

As a customer services adviser I am faced with quite a lot of negativity from the public which is reflected in my workplace which is also negative. It used to affect me and I was becoming more and more negative. This also affected the way I dealt with people. I receive many phone calls, it is just like a Call Centre and each call is different as every individual is unique and problems vary. I needed to find some way of dealing with these calls without it affecting me and of course the way I responded to the calls. I thought this was going to be difficult. However I was introduced to affirmations and visualisations along with effective breathing. These have helped me enormously. I can stay positive even when it is a difficult person on the phone. I am able to take time out before or after difficult calls to picture myself somewhere serene and calm. It only takes a couple of minutes but it really works. I am now eager to bring such positive techniques in to the workplace. I am slowly but surely getting some of my colleagues to try these techniques.

*I do not allow negative calls to upset me anymore.* Gill D. (Customer Services Manager).

*I work as a carer/therapist for children with special needs. I find this very satisfying but it is also challenging. I have to be able to communicate very effectively. It means being a good listener and taking time to listen carefully to find out what the children need. I am open to learning different techniques. Although I think I am someone who is very aware of myself and others I wanted to have this increased and extended. I already listen to relaxation CDs but discovered that the Qvolution visualisations particularly the clouds one let me look clearly and slowly at each of the floating clouds as they weaved and floated across the blue sky. Each time I try to see how much detail I can remember of the clouds. This helps extend my awareness. It is very effective both in my work and personal life.* Patricia-Ann M. (Carer).

*Using the ABC techniques have proved useful on many occasions. One of the most effective is the 'C' (creative imagery) visualisation technique which is really just a case of imagining yourself somewhere, some place where you feel good. Even looking at the different colours of everyday life and being more aware makes you realise that lots of things in life are good.* Walter T. (Web Designer/IT Consultant).

*I have recently taken the challenging step of leaving full time employment to go out on my own. I held a post in the financial sector which was extremely stressful. I know I was wealthy in the monetary sense but started to realise when doing the ABC techniques of this program that my life was not really 'wealthy' in the true sense. It was a huge step for me as I have always been employed. I am now in the transition period – really unemployed! until I decide what my options are. If it had not been for the affirmations and creative imagery exercises I would not even have taken this brave step. I am using the techniques more and more and am not afraid of what the future holds. I used to think I had no choices but I do and it is wonderful. I look forward to the future with confidence.* Cliff R. (ex Financial Services Chief Executive).

*Working for years in a very stressed environment I realised that I required techniques for remaining calm in all situations. After meeting the founder of Qvolution I started using the ABC techniques. I have also recently left my stressful job as HR and Health and Safety Director,* moving to Spain with my wife to start a new life. This was exciting but also frightening. The plans I had made for my future had to change and I used the creative imagery to picture myself in my new place, new job, new surroundings and in general having a fantastic time. I felt like a new person, stretching my boundaries, gliding effortlessly along imagining this to be my new life. Stuart M. (HR & H & S Director).

I am a regular client and work in a pressurised environment. For me there is nothing better than carrying out my positive affirmations and using creative imagery to make me feel better. I also do the breathing exercise and am already experiencing a new way of life. I feel much more positive about myself as I continue to use the ABC techniques. Peter F. (Business Adviser).

I like the breathing exercise which not only energises but relaxes me. I realise that some of my physical aches and pains are helped by a positive outlook. I have general problems as I take part regularly in sports but in addition to the breathing/relaxation exercises I find the use of ABC in combination helps me with motivation and self-esteem. John G (Sports coach).

I work often in traumatic areas attending accidents and incidents. I have not always found that counselling services offered after an incident is enough and it is usually for a very short period. I found the ABC techniques are better as I can use them on a regular basis and as they are offered online they are accessible 24/7 whenever I want or need. I think this could be of real assistance in every workplace. Andy D. (Fire Chief).

# The Five Shapes

Instructions

Look at the five shapes. Do NOT think about them. Spontaneously choose the two that you like the best. There is no hidden agenda. No-one is going to analyse you!

Now go back to chapter 5, section 5.2 and continue reading about How to find out who you are.

# INDEX

frustration 71

## H

habit, habits 63
habits 14, 58, 162
Health and Safety Management Standards for Stress, HSE Management Standards 69
Health & Safety 66
hearing visualisation 47
Holmes-Rahe Scale 74
Humanistic 9

## I

imagination 46, 49
Indian prana 50
inhalation 36
insecurity 123
inter-dependent 16

## J

Japanese ki 50
jealousy 16, 145
jealousy, possessiveness 121, 122, 123

## K

know how 13, 16, 139, 143

## L

labelling 94
laughter 23, 113, 114, 138

## M

Maslow, Abraham 26
mediation 107
meditation 32, 59

Lightning Source UK Ltd.
Milton Keynes UK
UKOW04f0619261114

242169UK00001B/8/P